The Birth of a Nation

...the ſin-offering, ... wh
...all the burnt-offering.
And the prieſt ſhall take of
... of the ſin-offering with
...and put it upon the horns
...altar of burnt-offering, and ſh
...all the blood thereof at t
...to the altar.
And he ſhall take away all t
...thereof, as the fat of the lamb
...away from the ſacrifice of t
...offerings; and the prieſt ſh
...them upon the altar, accordi
...offerings made by fire un
...: and the prieſt ſhall mak
...ment for his ſin that he ha
...mitted, and it ſhall be f

CHAP. V.

...ſaid unto me, Make us
...ſhall go before us: for a
...the man that brough
...of the land of Egypt, w
...is become of him.
...ſaid unto them, Whoſoever
...let them break it off.
...then I caſt it into
...there came out this calf.
...when Moſes ſaw that the
...were naked, (for Aaron had
...naked unto their ſhame
...enemies,)
...Moſes ſtood in the gate of
...and ſaid, Who is on the
...let him come unto me.
...the ſons of Levi gathered
...together unto him.
...he ſaid unto them, Thus
...LORD God of Iſrael, Put
...his ſword by his ſide,
...in and out from gate to gate
...the camp, and ſlay every
...brother, and every man his
...and every man his neigh-
...
...the children of Levi did
...to the word of Moſes: and
...of the people that day about
...and men.

...and he ſhall ſprinkle of the blood
...the ſin-offering upon the ſide of
...altar; and the reſt of the blood
...be wrung out at the bottom of
...altar: it is a ſin-offering.
And he ſhall offer the ſecond for
...burnt-offering, according to the
...er: and the prieſt ſhall make
...onement for him, for his ſin
...he hath ſinned, and it ſhall be
...ven him.
¶ But if he be not able to bring
...turtle-doves, or two young pi-
..., then he that ſinned ſhall bring
...offering the tenth part of an
...of fine flour for a ſin-offering;
...put no oil upon it, neither
...e put any frankincenſe there-
...it is a ſin-offering.
...hen ſhall he bring it to the
...and the prieſt ſhall take his
...as a memorial there-

...land flowing with milk
...for I will not go up in
...f thee; for thou art a
...people; leſt I conſume
...way.
...en the people heard theſe
...they mourned: and no
...on him his ornaments.
...LORD had ſaid unto
...unto the children of
...e a ſtiff-necked people:
...up into the midſt of
...ment, and conſume thee:
...w put off thy ornaments
...hat I may know what to
...children of Iſrael ſtrip-
...ves of their ornaments
...t Horeb.
...ſes took the tabernacle,
...it without the camp, afar
...camp, and called it The
...of the Congregation. And
...that every one which
...LORD went out unto the
D 5 tabernacle

The Birth of a Nation

Nat Turner and the Making of a Movement

Edited by Nate Parker

37INK

ATRIA

[illegible]oronto Sydney New Delhi

An Imprint of Simon & Schuster, Inc.
1230 Avenue of the Americas
New York, NY 10020

First 37 Ink/Atria Books hardcover edition September 2016

37INK / ATRIA BOOKS and colophon are trademarks of Simon & Schuster, Inc.

For information about special discounts for bulk purchases, please contact Simon & Schuster Special Sales at 1-866-506-1949 or business@simonandschuster.com.

The Simon & Schuster Speakers Bureau can bring authors to your live event. For more information or to book an event contact the Simon & Schuster Speakers Bureau at 1-866-248-3049 or visit our website at www.simonspeakers.com.

Interior design by Jason Snyder

Manufactured in the United States of America

10 9 8 7 6 5 4 3 2 1

Library of Congress Cataloging-in-Publication Data has been applied for.

ISBN 978-1-5011-5658-8
ISBN 978-1-5011-5659-5 (ebook)

For our children.
And our children's
children

CONTENTS

PART I

The Birth of a Movement

My Journey with Nat Turner

BY NATE PARKER

And I saw, and behold a white horse: and he that sat on him had a bow; and a crown was given unto him: and he went forth conquering, and to conquer.

—REVELATION 6:2 (KJV)

"How many of you know who Nat Turner is?" I wasn't the only one staring blankly at my African-American Studies professor. I'd overheard the name once or twice in my childhood, but without context—the where, the why, and the what of his story—his name had no resonance. My instructor paused a beat more before alleviating our curiosity. "Nat Turner led the most successful slave revolt in American history." The words "slave" and "revolt" in the same sentence seemed incongruent. He went on, "This revolt would not only send shock waves across this entire nation, but would aid in precipitating the American Civil War." I blinked back incredulity. Anyone who knew anything of American history knew enslaved Africans endured, but didn't dare fight. Anyone whose education mirrored my own knew it was benevolent Abe Lincoln who, following his moral compass, led this country to war, with the hope of freeing the slaves. This was what I had been taught, *facts* inscribed in the history books of my youth. If this Nat Turner truly existed, wouldn't he, too, have been in those same books? It made no sense. As confused as I was, it was my professor's next statement that rocked me the most. "This revolt . . . it took place in Southampton County, Virginia."

As the saying goes, you could have knocked me over with a feather. I grew up in Norfolk, Virginia, about forty-two miles east of Southampton County, Virginia. A decade of history courses and yet not once had there been a lesson, a lecture, or an assignment about the slave preacher, "General Nat"—the literate man of God who

A decade of history courses and yet not once had there been a lesson, a lecture, or an assignment about the slave preacher, "General Nat."

would engage in a holy war, sacrificing all he had to lead his people out of bondage. At that moment, I vowed to never again take another person's word regarding the narrative of my ancestors. It was then that I took hold of my miseducation and became hell-bent on untangling the twisted threads of its revisionist narrative. My independent study led me not only to Nat Turner but also to countless others who rose and fell in the name of liberation: Toussaint Louverture, Gabriel Prosser, Denmark Vesey, and Jean-Jacques Dessalines, to name a few. This desperate journey toward truth became my purpose, my North Star. It would not only serve in expanding my knowledge regarding this country's past, it would serve as the impetus of my desire to explore Nat Turner's life using the platform of film.

When I decided to produce a film on Nat Turner, I wanted to be very intentional about drawing parallels between the past and the present. I felt this would be the best way to provide context to many of the obstacles we face as I write with race in this country and in the entertainment industry. In society, there have been countless culprits responsible for both planting and spreading seeds of racial injustice. In film, all signals point to D.W. Griffith and his 1915 propaganda film *The Birth of a Nation.* This film was not only successful in influencing a massive swath of the country's population to embrace white supremacy as a form of self-preservation, it also laid a rock-solid foundation for this country's interracial affairs, one that still stands today. Set during the Civil War and Reconstruction, this film used carefully arranged moving images to tap deeply into the subconscious of an entire nation. In the wake of the film's release, we saw not only the resurgence of the near extinct Ku Klux Klan, but also the then president of the United States, Woodrow Wilson, hail the movie as a massive triumph. While studying this film, two things became immediately clear to me. First, that we are now harvesting the results of the seeds planted by Griffith all those years ago. And second, if we as an industry are to move forward, we must confront the injuries of our past. Reclaiming Griffith's title and repurposing it as a tool for progress and social justice was, in my mind, a good first step. The title, *The Birth of a Nation*, became a call to action, a challenge to all to "birth" a new nation of storytellers, truth speakers, and justice seekers. What Griffith used to hardwire, I would use to rewire. What he used for subjugation, I would use for liberation. I had a plan. I had a title. I had my hero. Yet I had no script.

When I began writing the script, I knew I wanted to present the story of a hero. I was less interested in the "typical" slave narrative, which hinges upon rampant victimization where the enslaved have little recourse. Instead, I wanted a story in which the

I wanted a story in which the hero clearly sees resistance as an option to overcoming his oppression.

hero clearly sees resistance as an option to overcoming his oppression. Brian Favors, an educator, wrote in reference to the film, "Individuals like Patrick Henry, known for his revolutionary ideals of 'liberty or death,' and William 'Braveheart' Wallace are deemed heroic because of their courage to pay the ultimate price for freedom against obstacles that are too frightening for most to confront. For people of African descent, who continue to experience racial oppression, cultural heroes are in short supply. Patrick Henry's belief that 'the great object is that every man be armed. Everyone who is able may have a gun,' was part of an American tradition that so revered freedom from

Griffith
Griffith
D. W. GRIFFITH
presents
The Birth of a Nation
Adapted from Thomas Dixon's novel
"The Clansman"
COPYRIGHT 1915 DAVID W. GRIFFITH CORPORATION
DG
Griffith
Griffith
¶ ". . . . The policy of the congressional leaders wrought . . . a veritable overthrow of civilization in the South . . . . . in their determination to 'put the white South under the heel of the black South.'"
WOODROW WILSON
DG
Griffith
Griffith
¶ The helpless white minority.
DG

Griffith
Griffith
¶ "The case was tried before a negro magistrate and the verdict rendered against the whites by the negro jury."
DG
Griffith
Griffith
¶ The riot in the Master's Hall.
¶ The negro party in control in the State House of Representatives, 101 blacks against 23 whites, session of 1871.
AN HISTORICAL FACSIMILE of the State House of Representatives of South Carolina as it was in 1870. After photograph by "The Columbia State."
DG
Griffith
Griffith
¶ "The white men were roused by a mere instinct of self-preservation ..... until at last there had sprung into existence a great Ku Klux Klan, a veritable empire of the South, to protect the Southern country."
WOODROW WILSON
DG

colonial oppression that the use of violence to resist was considered sacrosanct. His heroic declaration of 'give me liberty or give me death,' serves as a symbol of strength and sacrifice to white Americans who continue to utilize this battle cry to cultivate patriotism and pride. Unfortunately, black heroes who exhibit acts of courage in the face of racial oppression are rarely, if ever, acknowledged."

Inspired by the movie *Braveheart*, my goal was to create a heroic character whose trajectory bends toward resistance and ultimately triumph. This approach was especially significant to me for I had never encountered a film in which an African hero forcefully resisted. While I wanted to create material that would inspire hope, it was essential that the story line also be both incendiary and provocative. The creation of characters who are archetypically "good" or "bad" is an easy trap for a storyteller dealing with American slavery to fall prey to: Good and helpless black people are brutalized by demonic bad white people. This setup pits avaricious, sociopathic, and villainous whites against docile and impotent African victims who are being brought, helplessly, to the slaughter. This approach allows audience members to disassociate themselves from anyone with whom they cannot identify. They can avoid discomfort for the most part because they have no empathy for the characters. Benevolent *whites* think, "What kind of human being could do such a thing to another?" while across the aisles exhausted *blacks* exclaim, "I'm tired of seeing these slave movies."

With this in mind, I wanted to delve deeper into slavery and its infrastructure so that I could better understand the psychology of all of those who participated. My research, which involved social, economic, and political history, gave me deeper insight into the complexities of the times and these people who endured them. The more I studied, the more myths and mistruths I discovered from my childhood miseducation. I learned of the planter class and America's desperate dependency on chattel slavery to sustain and propel the country's economy. I learned just how far the tentacles of slavery reached: farther than the borders of the antebellum South, stretching deep into Northern states, Western territories, and even abroad. I learned of priests, churches, universities, and politicians—who were complicit in the buying, selling, and exploitation of African flesh. I learned about resilient enslaved Africans who survived and endured. I also learned about the enslaved who resisted; those who stood up to a system in which

they were routinely raped, murdered, and ripped from their families. This knowledge, newly excavated, but now firmly etched in my mind, decimated the images of the feeble and contented slaves I had previously possessed.

Armed with truth, I dove into the screenwriting process. One of the major goals I set from the beginning was to write the script in such a way that by the time Nat raised his axe, the audience, no matter their color or creed, would be in full support of him swinging it down on his oppressor. To do this I had to first present Nat as a human being. I had to liberate him from images and stories that sought to paint him as a terror-seeking, violent sociopath and reframe him as a man who was inspired by a desperate love for his God, his family, and his fellow captives. I had to show a man who *resorted* to violence, not out of a knee-jerk need for revenge, but as a last-ditch effort to deal with a system that was methodically destroying so many lives around him. I wanted the audience to be able to see the world as he saw it, challenging them to grapple with the everyday barrage of physical, spiritual, and emotional assault that permeated that world.

Beyond Nat's particular plight, it was also important to me that each secondary character carry his or her own specific drama; that each have a point of view that not only represented that character's position in society but also that character's unique and complex views and opinions regarding his or her environment and the systems that affected his or her everyday life—for better or worse. Juxtaposing these secondary characters' particular dilemmas with their relationship to our hero created all the stakes necessary to drive the narrative. In writing the character Samuel Turner, I wanted to veer away from creating a typical hillbilly slave owner. We've seen villains that love nothing more than spending their days ripping brown skin to shreds. By offering a character who, during his childhood, developed a genuine love for the movie's hero, my goal was to create a man and a relationship that was much more complicated. By dramatizing the moment when one friend inherits the other, I hope I provided insight into the ways in which the system corrupted everyone involved, even those who were well intentioned. As far as Samuel is concerned, we see how unchecked cognitive dissonance can rot a man's soul. Not only did I want his relationship with Nat to give insight into the social breakdown of this time period, I wanted it to have resonance even today. Far too often we attribute immorality and wrongdoing to individuals, rather than assessing

Nate studies his vision board during prep.

the environments that craft their behavior. My approach seems better suited to allow viewers to truly connect to Samuel Turner's quest to be a "good" slave owner, to let the audience take the journey with him as his best efforts are thwarted by a pervasively corrupt ecosystem.

Another noteworthy relationship is that of Nat and Cherry. What made this relationship particularly difficult to write was the nature of exploring love within the context of bondage. It was devastating to imagine being married to someone when neither you nor your spouse even so much as owned your own body. Yet for so many it was a reality. Not only did slaves not own their own bodies, they had no control over the safety of, or their proximity to, their loved ones. It was under these circumstances that Nat and Cherry exchanged vows and bore a child.

Religion is another theme I wanted to explore. I was particularly drawn to the dichotomy between the two groups—the enslaved and the enslavers, blacks and whites—both of whom worshiped a God of the same name, but had drastically opposed interpretations of The Word. For white Christians, the Bible was used, as Cherry says in the film, to subjugate, to "support our bondage." For black Christians, it was a source of hope and comfort.

In addition to dramatizing the tool and role of religion in the characters' lives, I also sought to create images that challenged Christian norms. I achieved this by starting the script with an African prologue, scripting a scene that would introduce African spirituality into Nat's life at an early age. Nat comes to know Christianity but only *after* he's embraced his African culture and heritage, which history tells us was revealed to him by his mother and grandmother, who maintained ties to their African traditions. As a result, Nat has the ability to see his faith, not as "the white man's religion," but as the pre-European, pre-colonial form of Christianity it has always been. It is my opinion that this tether to his heritage allowed him to better see how the individuals in his ecosystem were perverting the Christian faith and using it as an instrument of economic injustice and social control.

I also wanted to challenge contemporary religious norms depicting the afterlife. Jesus, God, and angels are most often portrayed as Europeans. So much so that as a young boy, I could not even call to my imagination an image of a non-European angel. By presenting the image of an African angel in the film, I hoped to provide a type of counterprogramming, a way in which the audience could also think more inclusively about spirituality or at least the iconography of spirituality.

Finally, one scene with religious overtones came from one of the facts about Nat's life that has survived. We know that Nat Turner was approached by a man named E. T. Brantley, who asked him to baptize him in repentance of his sins. Turner agreed. While imagining how shocking it must have been, at the time, to see this man of African descent baptize this man of European dissent, I was prompted to ask myself if I'd seen such an act. The sad realization was that I had not. At thirty-six years old, I had never seen a white man baptized by a black man. I thought the event was particularly dramatic and would not only serve as a powerful scene in the film but also open the viewer's mind to an act of faith seldom articulated in such an inclusive way.

I was particularly drawn to the dichotomy between the two groups . . . both of whom worshiped a God of the same name, but had drastically opposed interpretations of The Word.

Finally, I wanted to explore the aftermath of Nat's revolt, not just the punitive backlash, the tightening of restrictive legislation limiting the movement of the enslaved, the increase in the number of lynchings—but the progressive effects as well: the surge in acts of resistance following Nat's revolt, the rise in abolitionist political activity against the slaveholding states—all precipitating the Civil War. This serves particular significance because it thwarts the idea of the Turner revolt as an "isolated incident," giving life to the actual truth of the rebellion's impact, not only on the county, but on the entire country.

It's hard to describe the feeling I had when I finally wrote "Fade Out." So many tears on the page. The day I finished the first draft, I closed my laptop and prayed. I prayed for the humility to remain a servant to the project, that I would have the courage to commit to seeing it to its completion. While I knew many notes and drafts lay ahead, seeing those two words, *fade out*, gave me some peace. Nat Turner was, once again, alive and well.

I learned very quickly that writing that film and producing it were very different processes. While I knew I had a strong script, I also knew there would be massive obstacles in getting the project off the ground. From the self-perpetuating myth that the international market would reject a film with a lead of African descent, to the countless financial models that discourage the funding of films detailing the black experience—specifically one that presents a self-motivated African-American lead—these obstacles abounded.

In addition to the hurdles that are inherent in the system, there were others of a more complicated type. I'm thinking here of those presented not by outsiders but by my allies. Those well-intentioned individuals who, out of their desire to protect me, discouraged me from moving forward. I didn't blame them. The odds, laws, models, data, precedents (or lack thereof) define the rules of the game. Any hope to subvert those rules is immediately seen as futile. It became clear to me that these obstacles are precisely the stuff of which dreams are made. They're the lifeblood of the artist, in a way, at the risk of sounding lofty. So I had to push forward. Rather than think about the odds, I thought about and retreated into my faith and returned to the advice of those who had traveled this rocky ground before me. I kept going back to the words of George Lucas, who had directed me in *Red Tails*. When reflecting on his journey in getting *Star Wars* made, he said, "When people say it's impossible, that's how you know you're on the right track."

I caught my first major break after one particular dinner with a few industry people. When asked what I was working on, I launched into my pitch. One person asked if I had heard of the Sundance labs, referring to the screenwriting workshop held in Utah designed to support emerging writers. I had not. He offered to introduce me to the program director, Michelle Satter. I didn't know it then, but this was the single most important connection in my career up to that point. After an informal email introduction, I forwarded my script to Michelle. Within days, I received a call from her. This wasn't the first time I'd had an industry leader read the script. Usually, the feedback was along the lines of "This is an incredible script, but a bit too ambitious for a first-time director." Or "You should try to pursue something a bit more 'indie.'" Or, my favorite: "The script is fantastic. . . . Have you considered using it as a writing sample?" (a launchpad for other gigs). When I answered Michelle's call, the first words out of her mouth were "Nate, you definitely have something here, and I'm going to help make sure this gets made." Looking back, I can say this was the beginning, the first phase of bringing *The Birth of a Nation* to fruition.

For all of the support I received throughout this journey, it is safe to say Michelle Satter and the Sundance Institute proved most critical. Not just in the timing of their help, but for the key components offered during a massive lag in the progress of the project. Michelle quickly invited me into the Sundance fellowship program, which brought with it a much-needed grant. Within weeks, she had pulled me into the institute's high-level network, introducing me to some of the most respectable artists in the screenwriting space. Out of those connections came relationships with legendary screenwriter/directors Robin Swicord and James Mangold. I reached out to both of them and they responded immediately. Robin's nurturing approach led me to further explore Nat's inner arc. She engaged me in numerous exercises that challenged me to go deeper into his moment-to-moment thought process as he lived through those tumultuous times. These exercises served as the greatest tool in further developing Nat's character, motivation, and intentions. James, on the other hand, was like a hammer. He attacked the material, challenging any obvious tropes or triteness that stood in the way of good, unbiased storytelling. As the saying goes, if I only knew then what I know now. Often, in the filmmaking process, there is such an intense pressure and desire to get a project "made" that the script becomes an item on the checklist toward a green light, rather than the core of the process. Having professionals who have been consistently operating on the highest level of filmmaking put so intense a focus on the material was game-changing.

Another important lesson I've learned on this journey is that if you really want to achieve the seemingly impossible, something where you need others to join in your vision, you must have skin in the game. In an industry where financiers are conditioned to say no, you must be willing to find new and out-of-the-box ways to inspire people toward your vision. More often than not, this means taking risks. As I toured the town with the script in hand, articulating my passion, I could, at times, feel the momentum build. However, the moment I stepped away to take an acting job, I could see the energy dissipate. By having a foot in each world, it was if I were, however subconsciously, telling potential financiers (as well as myself) that I wasn't really serious. Here I was declaring this project to be the most important thing in my life, but not willing to set aside the security of my acting career to see it come to pass. Cue the out-of-the-box idea. I remember, clearly, that meeting with my team when I first informed them I was done acting, that the next skin I would live in would be that of Nat Turner. I knew what this meant. If I was wrong, twelve years of hard-fought, career-building progress could simply evaporate. I could lose the "relevancy" my team and I had worked so hard to obtain. While this declaration was in some ways terrifying, it was equally, if not more, liberating to disclose.

The watershed moment launched me into the next phase of my journey. I would spend the next several weeks turning down acting opportunities as I shifted my focus to setting and attending financing meetings full-time. My commitment to stepping away from other projects was met by a flood of unprecedented acting opportunities. Anxiety rose within my camp, followed by pressures to reconsider my radical position.

If ever there was a moment to quit, it would have been then. There was a ton of what I call "comfort money" on the table. People would have understood. Instead, I took my anxieties, my fears, and turned them toward my faith. Folded in prayer, I gave into the idea that as long as I was walking in what I believed to be the Lord's purpose for my life, it was okay to enter into a season of uncertainty.

While I hoped giving up my acting career would be enough, it was those first several financing meetings that showed me there was yet more skin to put in the game. I entered each meeting with what I believed to be very convincing arguments. I presented numbers and comparable models, painting clear pictures of opportunity. Still, no bites. Despite

I remember, clearly, that meeting with my team when I first informed them I was done acting, that the next skin I would live in would be that of Nat Turner.

all of my efforts to be seen as someone who had done the work, researched the odds, even quit his day job, I continued to be perceived as an actor with a script who wanted to be a director. It became painfully obvious that I needed to walk into these rooms with something more tangible. I needed to do the one thing artists are always discouraged from doing. I needed to financially share the risk. I needed to put in money of my own. At the time, this seemed to be the only way to convince financiers I was serious. After a long conversation with my wife (my best friend and rock throughout this process), I was given permission to dip into our savings. Now, armed with my own money, I first invested in a world-class production designer and engaged with location scouts around film communities in the South. We looked at Virginia, North Carolina, South Carolina, Louisiana (skipping Mississippi due to their flying of the Confederate flag) before we settled on Savannah, Georgia. With its well-preserved plantation homes, proximity to vast and picturesque swampland, and competitive tax incentives, it quickly became the standout choice. I immediately flew there with my production designer at the time, Wynn Thomas, to start what would be a tremendously effective scouting effort. We were able to capture countless pictures and video snippets of locations that, for the most part, would become the actual places in which we would shoot the film.

Armed with a database of visuals, I created a visual pitch book that would become the basis of my presentation. To that presentation, I would add a mood reel—a short video narrative intercutting scenes from films within the genre. Not only did this give me tangible assets, but it also provided me with a massive boost of confidence, which I needed when I was called to stand in front of those with the resources to make this project a reality. While a major part of my financing pitch revolved around data, pictures, and presentation, the most important component dealt with legacy.

It says in the Bible, "A good man leaves an inheritance to his children's children." That verse has always stayed with me. What do I owe my children's children? What will I leave behind that, once in their hands, will elevate their experience as human beings on this planet? Of all the things I would consider my talents or gifts, how many of those things will translate into something that serves my community and mankind for the better? These were the same questions I posed to my potential financiers. "When you are dead and gone, and your children are asked who you were, what you stood for and what you did—how will they respond? Will they say he left me money? Or will they be able to point to something more intentional—a veritable attempt to push humanity forward." In presenting the project as a legacy-based opportunity, one in which I was myself invested, we created opportunities for aspirational synergy.

While many of the industry's financiers were in Hollywood, I quickly learned that to successfully raise the amount I needed, I would have to expand my search outside of the film community. It was time to start reaching out to high-net-worth individuals. A quick scroll through my contacts, however, revealed I didn't know many. I reached out to a friend and director who was gracious enough to offer me a list of financiers he had compiled during the journey to getting his own film made. Thus began the phase of what that director calls "kissing frogs." Without hesitation, I attacked the list, cold calling more than one hundred random people. In addition, I reached out to former classmates from college, former business colleagues and collaborators, and old friends, asking if they knew people who might be interested in "diversifying" investments within the film industry. As I dialed number after number, I couldn't help but be reminded of

"When you are dead and gone, and your children are asked who you were, what you stood for and what you did—how will they respond?"

my telemarketing days as a teen. I sold accidental death and dismemberment insurance by phone—at least I attempted to. I can still hear the voice of my twentysomething boss ringing out across the cubicles: "Remember. Every 'no' is just one step closer to your 'yes.'" Who knew how useful his advice would be years later.

Eventually, I brought on a few producers, and they aided in setting up rooms in which I could pitch. I swapped the phone for the conference table. After what seemed like a million frogs, a few princes began to emerge. Those early investors ranged from NBA stars to real estate moguls and documentary filmmakers. However, as we neared our target raise, we encountered another stumbling block. Just months from our target prep date, a massive chunk of financing dropped out. With so many pieces in motion, I sprinted to fill the hole. Armed with determination and mountain-moving faith, I decided to revisit a close friend and hedge fund manager who had already formally passed on the project. He was having a fiftieth birthday party in New York City, so I jumped on a plane from Los Angeles to New York and prepared myself for one final ask. I'm not sure if he could see the need in my eyes or if he was just in a good mood, but this time he said yes without hesitation. He went on to explain that he wasn't interested in investing in the film but he would invest in me. He said, "I might just be putting my money in a hole and setting it on fire, but I want to see you win." When it was all said and done, he would commit the largest chunk of equity in the entire pool.

He said, "I might just be putting my money in a hole and setting it on fire, but I want to see you win."

Even now, I look back at that trip as critical. Had he said no, I believe, the film might have fallen apart. I headed back to Los Angeles on a cloud. However, the plane had no sooner landed than I was forced back to earth. Other investors, having learned of the initial withdrawal of funds, got cold feet and retreated. This left us again with a hole in the raise. Fortunately, my agency came through, introducing me to a financier and producer who would not only become a close friend but would also provide the second miracle in sealing our financing raise.

Finally, we had the money committed. It was time to start spending. Not so, I learned. In the independent film world, projects, especially those marked as wildcards, as ours was (first-time director, actor directing himself, overambitious schedule, overambitious script, shoestring budget), financiers often request a bond company to insure delivery of the film. In this particular context, even with all of the money committed, we could not start our spend until the funds sat in an escrow account. This would be fine if all parties funded right away. But this was not the case. As the closings for the financing labored on, one of my costars, one who had been with me for more than a year and had turned down other jobs in the meantime, was being pushed into a time pickle. If we didn't fund

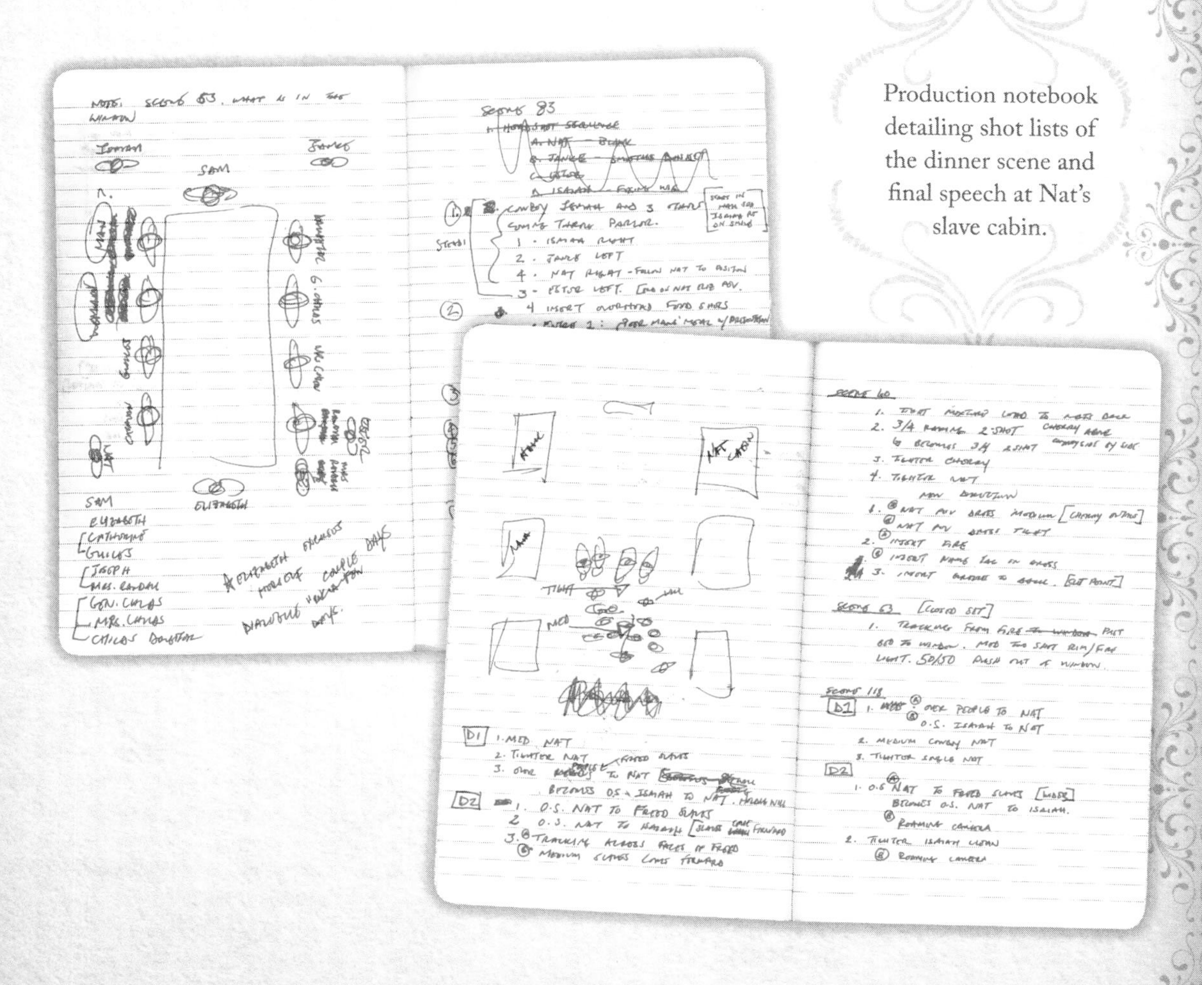

Production notebook detailing shot lists of the dinner scene and final speech at Nat's slave cabin.

within those next few weeks, we would lose him. In a final act of reckless faith, I asked my wife if we could spend our last bit of savings to move our family to Savannah. She supported the idea and we soon found ourselves heading to Georgia. (Yes, my wife is a saint.) Upon our arrival, I reached out to my financiers with a single statement: "I'm in Savannah. I am in prep and would love for you to join me." My first AD, Dutch Deckaj, immediately hopped in his Jeep and met me there. He said, "No director of mine will be in prep by himself." Others followed, including my line producer, Mark Moran; costume designer, Francine Jamison-Tanchuck; and beyond. Those first couple of days, we found ourselves packed into a motel kitchenette in "prep." What followed in the coming days was truly miraculous. Financiers, led by my friend the hedge fund manager, began to lend us money to keep us afloat. Within a week, we would witness the fastest closing of money into escrow that any of our producers had ever seen.

From the start I knew I wanted to direct this film, but that doesn't mean I was without some fears. I am disciplined by nature and had a sense of how I wanted to direct the movie, the effects I wanted to achieve, but I had no experience. Yes, I'd been an actor in a few films, witnessing firsthand and up close a variety of directors run sets, but I had little real-world, hands-on experience. Determined to shake my anxiety, I decided the best way to gain the wisdom I lacked was to seek it in others. My first call was to my close friend Spike Lee. He responded immediately, inviting me to New York to discuss the project. He not only offered script notes and advice from personal experience, he also came to Los Angeles to give me notes and thoughts on my very first cut. I also reached out to Mel Gibson. Having done both *Braveheart* and *Apocalypto*, and having directed himself in the former, Mel Gibson could offer invaluable advice. He, too, responded immediately, inviting me to his office in Santa Monica for what would become a three-hour-plus meeting. He spoke about the importance of rest and how my health was my greatest asset. He would go on to make himself available over the course of the next two months, even calling me the day before I shot my battle sequences to lend last words of encouragement. I reached out to Steven Soderbergh, who is known as one of the most efficient directors in town. He invited me to his set in New York while filming *The Knick*. He offered many wise words, including "Know what you want and know when you have it." He stressed the importance of preparation and decisiveness, words that no doubt strengthened my leadership throughout the process. I reached out to Edward Zwick, director of *Glory* and *Defiance*. Ed walked me through battle scenes, shot by shot. We discussed technical components such as angles, planes, and composition. He also was extremely helpful in making strategic edits to make the script shootable, given the ambitious schedule. These are just a few of the many ways artists of the highest caliber reached out to support me in the making of this film. While I started the journey having no formal film school education, I arrived in Savannah feeling I had not arrived alone.

"Know what you want and know when you have it."

When I tell people who've seen the film that I had twenty-seven days to shoot it, I can see the shock wash over their faces. Then they always ask, "How did you pull it off?" Mostly, I attribute our execution to a motivated crew and cast, who stood with me through every twist and turn, elevating me at times when I felt I would fall. I must be clear: Nothing good in this business happens from the work of one person. Collaboration at every level is a critical component in achieving the impossible. Such was true for this film. I communicated very early on to my team that in order to pull this off we would have to be in perfect sync. We would have to understand that our sole motivation in this endeavor would be to serve the project at any and all costs. Buying into this concept would prove paramount in eliminating ego and establishing a collective consciousness and goal. This meant organizing countless meetings, early on, where thoughts, fears, concerns, and ideas could be presented. The idea that his or her opinion mattered seemed to empower each crew member. It also allowed me to articulate the specifics of my vision in a way that promoted clarity and laid the foundation for my expectations. I wanted to create an environment where people understood that they were hired for their talent but that they also had agency to trust their instinct at every turn. Given the blistering pace we faced, there was little time for rhetoric and deliberation. Decisions had to be made swiftly. I had absolutely no intention of micromanaging my crew, and I told them that early on. As a director friend once advised, "Hire the best, and get out of the way." Articulating the importance of the project, what would be required to deliver it, and my reliance on their talent, primed the crew to do their best possible work.

This same approach rang true for the cast. Rehearsals, early in prep, aided in setting the tone for the shoot. I had worked with researchers to compile a study packet for each actor. These packets were geared toward each performer's specific character, covering everything from the time period and social trends to the political climate. The goal was to introduce each actor to the life of the character in a real way and to be open to feedback and discourse around making each of them comfortable in the skin he or she would inhabit during those next months.

As a director friend once advised,
"Hire the best, and get out of the way."

Not everything in prep dealt with cast and crew. Due to our budgetary restrictions and ambitious shooting schedule, the bond company was watching us very carefully. While we were off to a great start in terms of prep, a huge stumbling block was tossed at our feet. Because we arrived in Savannah at a time when most of the local crew had been hired away on other jobs, we had to make more out-of-state hires than previously anticipated. This seemingly small issue ate into nearly a third of our contingency budget, which quickly triggered a red flag for the bond company. So there I was, before shooting even a foot of film, sitting with my bond rep. As kind and supportive as he'd been up to this moment, he had a job to do. In no uncertain terms, he informed me about how far into our contingency budget we had dipped and what it could mean for me and the film if I didn't rein it in: I could not afford to go into overtime; I could not afford to miss making a day; I could not afford to lose a day to weather. For a first-time director—who was not only directing but also acting—this felt like the kiss of death. Preparing me for the worst, the bond rep suggested we have a follow-up sit-down at the completion of the first two weeks of shooting. Working under the assumption I'd be behind, he told me to be prepared to cut scenes, cut locations, and cut days. Simply put,

if I fell short, the shoot would have to change drastically. Understanding his position, I agreed to being open to restructuring if I were to fall behind. In a bit of a bold move, I met him with a counter deal: "If I do make my days, avoid overtime, and don't get rained out, there are a few things I will need in return." I asked if he would allow me to expand the budget a small amount to include a technocrane and a significantly larger number of extras for my final "gallows" sequence. With little hesitation, he agreed and the deal was made. Two weeks into shooting, I received a call. It was my bond rep, and the emotion in his voice was one of relief. The technocrane was put to good use and a few more local extras were employed.

The actual shooting of the film, technically, proved to be a highlight of the experience. That began with the cinematography, which was extremely important to me from the very beginning. By the time I started my search for a cinematographer, I had a pretty clear idea of the direction in which I wanted to go. I pulled inspiration from many filmmakers, ranging from Alfred Hitchcock to Stanley Kubrick, Orson Welles, Spike Lee, and Akira Kurosawa; developed an image board of shot angles and another of color palette in tone; and pulled stills from more contemporary films like *The Assassination of Jesse James* and *The Iron Lady*. In addition, I watched countless films, all with the goal of identifying cinematographers. That search brought me, very quickly, to Elliot Davis. Examining his work, which included *The Iron Lady* and *The Man of Tai Chi*, I was particularly drawn to his use of lighting and shadows to establish tone and mood. Between that and his cool color palettes and his excellence in both heavy camera moves and dynamic handheld shots, I was sold. Elliot and I would spend six hours each day of prep storyboarding, shot listing, and exploring the best ways to promote an "economy of filmmaking." By the time we arrived on set, we'd shot-listed the film twice through and had driven our average setups to below ten per scene. I would also shot-list once more through on my way to the set, focused on eliminating at least one more setup per scene. By the time we arrived on set, so many of our questions were answered. We didn't have to think any more about where we would put the camera or how much coverage we needed. We were in lockstep, and this always made the set feel active and productive. Our preparation, coupled with the brilliance in which my first AD, Dutch, ran the set, kept us on time and on budget.

The end of principal photography proved to be an overwhelming experience. I slept for nearly a week straight before getting back to work. Knowing I had it all "in the can," my only worry was getting it safely back to Los Angeles for the edit. I'll be honest in saying that at this point, I still had no idea if I had the film I'd envisioned. The dailies looked great, but until I had a cohesive edit, I'd be in the dark. Someone once told me, "The edit is the last rewrite." I'd captured so many images, so many thoughts, but the collaboration between me and an editor was yet to be executed. As with my previous searches for crew members, I was set on finding an editor with experience in the genre and the tone I was seeking. With films like *Braveheart* and *Glory* under his belt, legendary editor Steven Rosenblum became my target. By now, you could guess, we had very little money. In fact, any offer we could make, in the face of Steve's quote, would be nothing short of offensive. After sending Steve the script, I told my line producer to do everything he could to get me on the phone with him. Our first conversation resulted in a pass. He loved the script but could not commit to what we were offering. So I called him again the next day. Then I called him the next day, and the next day. That "no" became a "Nate, I can't." That "I can't" became "maybe." That "maybe" became "yes."

Progression of makeup by Douglas Noe
for the gallows scene.

And that yes catapulted our project into a place we never would have achieved without Steve. In fact, after viewing his first assembly cut, I could hardly speak. It was the first moment I realized the impact potential of the film.

The edit, in so many ways, set the tone for the rest of post-production, the most emotional part being the scoring. Before I met Henry Jackman, I had only two songs I knew had be a part of the film's score. Nina Simone's version of "Strange Fruit" was the first. The other was a song I first heard when visiting the Historically Black Colleges and Universities (HBCU) Wiley College in Marshall, Texas, where, after having worked with the college on my previous project, I had committed to help develop their scholarship program using my platform as an artist. On this particular visit, which happened to be in 2010, their a cappella choir, which is among the best in the country, sang a song that rocked me to my core. At the song's conclusion, I approached the choir and the conductor, Dr. Hayes, to inform them of a film I was developing, a biopic on Nat Turner. I told them that this song, "I Couldn't Hear Nobody Pray," would, no doubt, be the song that closed my film. With these two songs in place, Henry and I collaborated to develop a score that would complement these pieces while supporting the film with a unique combination of African and orchestral movements. A major part of the score, as I heard it in my head, should be performed with voice. Nat Turner's journey throughout the film was laced with tremendous highs and lows. Because he was so in tune with his faith, it seemed right that there be a sonic representation of his journey that emulated the voices of angels. When Nat experiences pain, we should hear the angels' voices sharing his pain. When he stands in courage, we should hear their voices rising in approval. With this in mind, Henry wrote choral arrangements that serve as these angelic responses to Nat's journey. These angelic voices were sung by none other than the Wiley College a cappella choir.

It seems like so much has happened since we wrapped our twenty-seventh day. I remember that feeling of accomplishment and love that permeated the entire set. Some passed around champagne, others light beer, as hugs, tears, and smiles continued through the night. I watched it all, wearing my own wide smile. A group of people had come together, galvanized around the hope of creating a piece of art that could somehow positively affect our industry, our country, and ultimately the world.

"And above all, clothe yourselves with love, which binds us all together in perfect harmony."

It is my hope and prayer that you all leave this film activated. That words like healing, resistance, self-determination, faith, equality, and justice will find a useful place in your daily vocabulary. That we all, collectively, have a riotous disposition toward injustice. That we use our occupational, social, and technological tools to rise up against any injustice that exists in our daily ecosystem. That we take personally any assault on the human body, mind, or spirit—whether it be directed at ourselves or others. That we reject apathy and embrace possibility. That we rebuke indifference and exercise empathy.

PART II

A History of Resistance

The Unbroken Chain of Enslaved African Resistance and Rebellion

BY ***ERICA ARMSTRONG DUNBAR*** *AND* ***DAINA RAMEY BERRY***

INTRODUCTION

On October 2, 1831, Nat Turner turned thirty-one years old. It was a Sunday, perhaps the most important day of the week for this deeply religious man who typically spent his Sabbath in deep prayer and meditation. But this Sabbath and birthday would be different from all others. Turner did not celebrate the day of his birth with friends or family, nor did he preach to the enslaved men and women who lived on the Travis farm in Southampton County, Virginia. He was in hiding, and knew that it was just a matter of time before he was captured and forced to answer for his actions.

He hid in a makeshift den—a simple depression in the ground that was covered by old fence rails. His cracked lips and hollow stomach reminded him on his birthday morning that he had spent the last forty days in an earthen coffin. It was only the human body's need for water and food that pulled him away from his hideout. His stiffened body moved without detection in the dead of night, in search of water from a nearby pond and provisions from local farm homes. He avoided capture for more than two months.

Turner had orchestrated the most powerful act of resistance—a slave insurrection that would become one of the most notorious rebellions in the history of the United States. At its end, close to sixty white men, women, and children lay dead. In the rebellion's immediate aftermath, hundreds of black people would pay the ultimate price. Their tortured and slaughtered bodies absorbed the anger and fear of white slaveholders, serving as a cautionary tale for any other future black rebels.

The rebellion was not an oddity or a spontaneous reaction to personal circumstance. Instead, this was a carefully planned and executed attack against the institution of American slavery that by 1830 had claimed more than two million souls. Turner's rebellion was a powerful example of black resistance, and a reminder that black people fought, and would continue to fight, against the system that labeled them human chattel. Beginning with the moment they were kidnapped and stolen from their homelands, black men, women, and children resisted—sometimes in calculated and elaborate ways that involved maps and tools, and other times with slow and barely noticeable opposition. And on occasion, violence begat violence, as enslaved people committed assault, arson, and murder. The mere act of survival *was* resistance.

OPPOSITE TOP
Depiction of the slave trade and the town of Mombassa.

OPPOSITE BOTTOM
Illustration showing deck plans and cross sections of the British slave ship *Brookes*.

The film *The Birth of a Nation* and this essay follow a similar tradition of black resistance. By sharing the stories of Nat Turner, Gabriel Prosser, and Osborne Anderson in Virginia; Denmark Vesey and Jemmy in South Carolina; Lear Green in Maryland; and David Walker in Massachusetts, we continue the work of reframing American history. This essay highlights only a few clear moments of resistance within centuries of this black freedom struggle. These stories dismantle the mythology of complacent slavery—the image of enslaved men and women who were too docile or timid to fight the evils of human bondage. From the arson in New York, to the beating drums of the Stono Rebellion, and the marching in New Orleans, blacks fought for their freedom and found it via conspiracy and insurrection, in their faith, in literacy, in mutiny and escape, and ultimately in death. Their stories tell us in the most unapologetic and clear fashion that oppression always meets with reactive and proactive resistance.

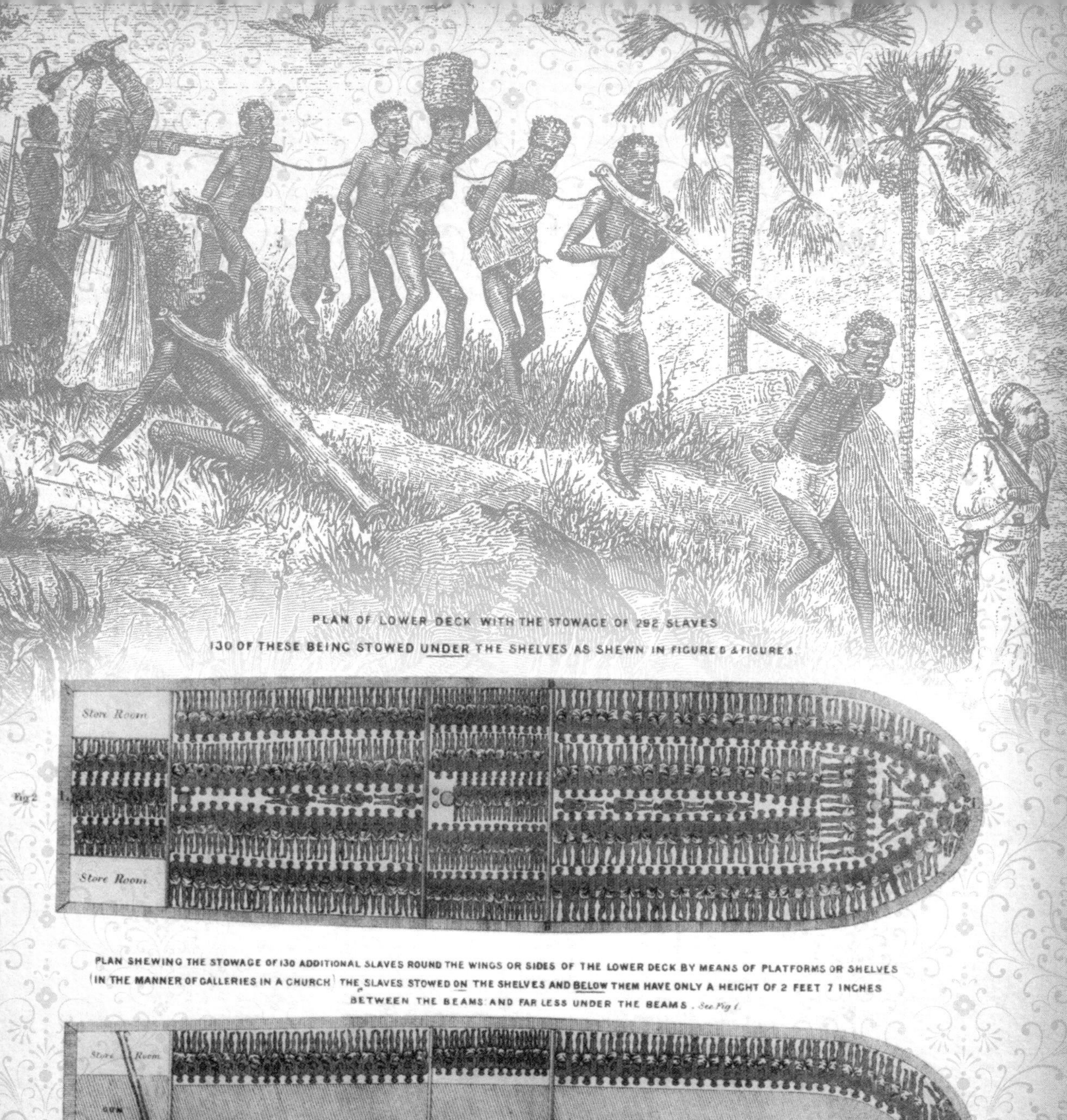
PLAN OF LOWER DECK WITH THE STOWAGE OF 292 SLAVES
130 OF THESE BEING STOWED UNDER THE SHELVES AS SHEWN IN FIGURE 6 & FIGURE 5.
Store Room
Fig 2
Store Room
PLAN SHEWING THE STOWAGE OF 130 ADDITIONAL SLAVES ROUND THE WINGS OR SIDES OF THE LOWER DECK BY MEANS OF PLATFORMS OR SHELVES
(IN THE MANNER OF GALLERIES IN A CHURCH) THE SLAVES STOWED ON THE SHELVES AND BELOW THEM HAVE ONLY A HEIGHT OF 2 FEET 7 INCHES
BETWEEN THE BEAMS: AND FAR LESS UNDER THE BEAMS. See Fig 1.

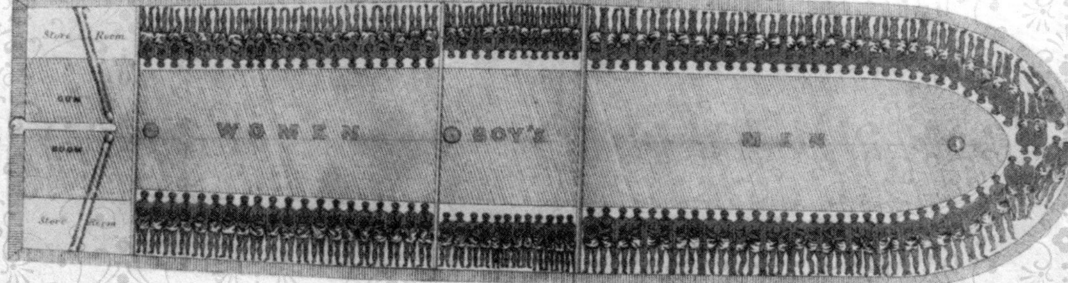
Store Room
GUN
ROOM
Fig 3
WOMEN
BOY'S
MEN

We will never know exactly how many Africans were stolen from their homelands. Some historians suggest that more than fifteen million men, women, and children were kidnapped, tortured, branded, and shuttled onto disease-ridden ships anchored off the coast of western Africa. Once the ships set sail, Africans lay chained in the most degraded of conditions, enduring a Middle Passage that deposited them in the Caribbean, the jaws of Atlantic world slavery. A smaller number of kidnapped Africans, near five hundred thousand, were forced to survive another voyage, one that landed them on the shores of the English colonies in America. In 1619, twenty Africans arrived in Jamestown, Virginia, and were sold as servants into an America that had not yet clearly defined black slavery. These Africans, and the ones who would follow in their footsteps, watched Virginia and the other colonies prosper from black labor as tobacco, rice, indigo, and other cash crops strengthened America's economy. Massachusetts was the first colony in America to legalize African slavery, an institution that spread like contagion through the English empire in America.

TO SET FIRE

Africans held on to memories of their homelands and passed down their traditions from one generation to the next, always looking for an opportunity to reinstate what they believed they were owed: liberty. Although outnumbered in most of the colonies, Africans plotted and conspired to gain their freedom. The steady stream of slaves from the Caribbean carried news of slave rebellion in Jamaica and Antigua, stories that reminded all who conspired in the American colonies that they were not alone in their intentions. Slave insurrection terrified white colonists, and in April of 1712 the fears of New York slaveholders became a reality.

By the early 1700s, one out of every five residents in New York was enslaved, and on April 6, 1712, twenty-three slaves, armed with guns and hatchets, met in an orchard and set fire to a slaveholder's house. Violence erupted, nine whites were killed, and six others were injured. Militia units put down what was called the first slave insurrection in colonial America. They arrested scores of black people and sent twenty-one Africans to be executed. Shocked and horrified, white colonists tightened the laws in New York, making arson a crime that was punishable by death. This rebellion would not be the last time that Africans and their descendants fought the oppression of slavery with guns, knives, and fire. It was the birth of a tradition of resistance that refused to die, as long as slavery lived.

TO BEAT DRUMS

Jemmy may not have known about the rebellion in New York. Twenty-seven years had passed since the uprising, and he lived seven hundred miles away, just outside Charleston, South Carolina. Jemmy had been kidnapped from Africa and was likely Congolese or Angolan. He probably learned to speak both Portuguese and Spanish, and in addition to learning how to read, he listened carefully to the hushed stories of slave rebellion in the South Carolina colony where blacks outnumbered whites two-to-one. While he may not have known about the insurrection in New York, he most certainly knew about Spanish Florida's free black town, Gracia Real de Santa Teresa de Mose. Although it was located almost three hundred miles away, Jemmy knew that black fugitives had found freedom in

Tired of abuse and ready to die for their freedom, close to one hundred slaves joined Jemmy and his comrades as they marched toward Spanish Florida.

this newly established town. For Jemmy and the thousands of slaves who lived in South Carolina and Georgia, Florida represented hope, an escape from the degraded life of enslavement. During the early morning hours of Sunday, September 9, 1739, Jemmy and some twenty slaves gathered near the Stono River, discussed their plan, and broke into a local store/warehouse in order to arm themselves with guns and powder.

The group marched south, raiding homes and killing slave owners. And as they traveled, they collected more recruits. Tired of abuse and ready to die for their freedom, close to one hundred slaves joined Jemmy and his comrades as they marched toward Spanish Florida.

The marchers beat drums, and cries of "Liberty!" came from the mouths of the growing rebel force. Their momentum continued, and death came quickly to the unfortunate whites who crossed their path. A white innkeeper was spared because he "was a good man and kind to his slaves," but the exceptions were few.

The band of slaves advanced, vowing to let nothing stand in their way. But their will could not overpower mounted and armed slave owners who pursued them. By nightfall, some of the rebel slaves had been wounded, captured, or killed, but it would take almost a week for a white militia to catch most of the rest of those who had fled. Jemmy and his comrades killed close to thirty whites in this full-scale revolt against slavery. Forty-four blacks were executed or killed; some were shot to death, others were hanged. Only one of the marchers was able to escape—he remained at large for three years but was eventually found and immediately hanged.

The Stono Rebellion set off alarm bells throughout the colonies. In an attempt to preempt any other slave insurrections, the South Carolina Assembly passed the Negro Act of 1740, a law that limited the lives of blacks and native people, all of whom were to be considered slaves. There were many restrictions written into this new law, such as forbidding slaves to assemble in large groups, to use loud instruments such as drums, and to learn to write English. The Negro Act was a reminder to white slaveholders across the colonies that in order for African slavery to continue, black people must be controlled.

TO BURN AGAIN

But there was no foolproof plan that could suppress the anger and the will of enslaved people. A year after the Negro Act was passed, black slaves were at it again. But this time there would be no band of armed marchers. Instead, fire was the weapon of choice. On Wednesday, March 18, 1741, the lieutenant governor of New York watched his mansion within the walls of Fort George burn to the ground. Initially, New Yorkers presumed the fire to be accidental, but over the course of a few short weeks, ten fires were set across the city, destroying property and the peace of mind of slave owners.

Rumors spread that the arson was the work of angry slaves, with a plan to burn down the city and to murder every white person. A manhunt began in haste, and over the course of the spring and summer of 1741, 152 enslaved and free black New Yorkers were arrested. Caesar Varick, Prince Auboyneau, and Cuffee Philipse were the alleged masterminds, accused by a sixteen-year-old white maidservant of plotting the entire affair. One of the accused chose to slit his own throat rather than face punishment by the hands of his captors. Eighty men and one woman admitted to their involvement, and according to the confessions of the alleged arsonists, they planned not only to murder white colonists, but to also depose the governor of New York. They would replace him with a black man. This would never happen.

But this time there would be no band of armed marchers. Instead, fire was the weapon of choice.

Thirteen people were burned at the stake and seventeen went to the gallows. Two hanging black bodies were left to bloat and rot in public, a reminder of the steep consequences of a failed rebellion. Eighty-four men and women were removed from the colony and sold into the death grip of slavery in the Caribbean. No one knows what happened to those who made the reverse trip back to the islands. They most likely did not live to witness what would be the greatest slave insurrection on record. It was a rebellion that secured black freedom for a Caribbean colony and gave birth to the first free black republic of the western hemisphere. Her name was Haiti.

TO REVOLT

The Caribbean islands were pockmarked with constant revolts and slave resistance as men and women escaped the cruelest of conditions. Those who could fled to the maroon communities of the mountains and forests; others stole livestock, physically fought with their owners, and looked for any and every way to end the bone-crushing labor of sugar and coffee production. Toussaint Louverture was born into this world of Caribbean

Toussaint Louverture was the leader of the Haitian independence movement, the most successful slave revolt in modern history.

slavery, in Saint-Domingue, but lived closely with relatives who came from Africa. They reminded Louverture that his roots were those of a free African, no matter his imposed status by French slave owners. Once he procured his freedom, Louverture became an experienced soldier and led enslaved comrades on a journey that would end their bondage and become a symbol of black resistance around the world. In August of 1791, the slaves and free people of color rose in rebellion against their French captors. The rebellion was fierce and lasted for more than a decade, but freedom would not be denied. Even after the capture and imprisonment of Louverture in 1803, the fight did not end until January 1, 1804, when the Republic of Haiti was born.

All who read the newspapers, and even those who didn't, concluded one thing: Slavery could be and was destructible. Haiti's slave rebellion reminded Americans that black freedom could be won, an uplifting symbol for black slaves and a terrifying one for white slave holders.

While the Caribbean was in an uproar, the turn of a new century in the United States marked the expansion of slavery into new territories. Planters in Maryland, Virginia, and the Carolinas looked for fresh soil to plant and produce cotton, sugar, and rice. Land that had been exhausted from tobacco production pushed farmers to move farther south and west. They migrated and set up homes in new states such as Alabama, Louisiana, and Texas. Change also brought new technologies such as cotton gins, printing presses, and railroad lines. These innovations helped perfect crops, print newspapers, and transport goods and people to faraway places. Enslaved people felt the brunt of these changes as many of the changes centered on the continued exploitation of their labor.

TO PLOT

Just as cotton spread across the South, so too did plans for black rebellion. Enslaved men and women knew about the hard-fought war for black liberation in the Caribbean, and they had witnessed American colonists win their independence from British rule. The feel of revolution was simply palpable, and on a farm in Henrico County, Virginia, an enslaved man named Gabriel Prosser seized the opportunity to revolt. He was born in 1776, on the eve of the Revolution, and by the turn of the nineteenth century, Prosser was six feet two inches tall and a skilled blacksmith who could both read and write. In September of 1799, he was found guilty of stealing a pig and assaulting a white man, crimes that led Prosser to a public branding and a month in jail. It was at this moment that Prosser decided he would be a slave no more. He began to plan and believed that if slaves stood up, demanded their rights, and rebelled, poor whites would join them in their revolt. Prosser planned to take hold of Capitol Square in Richmond and to hold the governor hostage in order to bargain with authorities. Over time, Prosser collected close to thirty men, both enslaved and free, who stood ready to fight for freedom.

Prosser announced that the rebellion would take place on August 30, 1800, and their plans included capturing Norfolk and Petersburg. However, a violent rainstorm postponed the revolt, allowing enough time for a few slaves to buckle under the pressure of what was to come. Once their owners were informed of the plot, white patrols and state militia scoured the countryside and rounded up suspected conspirators. Prosser remained at large for more than two weeks but was eventually captured aboard a schooner in Norfolk. The trials of the suspected conspirators lasted almost two months, and at their close, twenty-six slaves were executed and a number of slaves were sold out of state, most likely to the new and expanding lower South. Some of these men might have ended up in Louisiana, where slavery would once again be challenged in the bloodiest of ways.

TO MARCH

Charles Deslondes knew about revolution. He had been born into slavery in Haiti and was quickly shuttled to the Louisiana Territory by a slave owner who feared the worst. During the Haitian Revolution, he saw the terror on the faces of whites who fled from their homes with whatever possessions they could carry, including their human property. Deslondes had earned his new owner's trust and was assigned the notorious job of overseer. Using his close connection to the slaves on the German Coast of Louisiana, he plotted with them, using the same techniques as had Jemmy and Gabriel. On January 8, 1811, Deslondes led a small band of slaves into the home of a white planter, wounded the slave owner, and murdered his son. Deslondes and his followers desperately searched the home for weapons in preparation for the fight of their lives. After arming themselves, they dressed in militia uniforms.

They marched for close to three days to New Orleans, beating drums and crying

There would be no trial for Deslondes.

out for liberty. They burned farms and destroyed livestock on their way to meet with other black revolutionaries in the port city. Deslondes watched the number of followers swell from several dozen into the hundreds. Reports of the black insurrection prompted federal troops and private militias to respond with crushing severity, and by January 11, Deslondes and his five hundred followers were outgunned. No one knows how many black lives were lost in the aftermath of the rebellion. Eighteen men were tried and executed by firing squad. Just like the Stono Rebellion insurgents', their bodies were decapitated and placed on public display. There would be no trial for Deslondes. Once captured, the rebel leader watched as his hands were severed from his arms. He was shot multiple times and beaten to death. His dead body was set ablaze.

TO PREACH

The consequences for violent resistance were known by all, but for some, rebellion began not with a gun, but with a book—the Bible. By the 1820s, hundreds of thousands of black men and women had adopted Christianity, often combining their ancestral beliefs in Islam and indigenous religions with their faith in a New Testament and Jesus Christ. Such was the case with Telemaque, better known as Denmark Vesey.

He would become a South Carolinian preacher, but like Deslondes, he knew the

He must have believed that it was the grace of God that brought him the most cherished blessing—his freedom.

intimacies of slavery in the Caribbean. Born sometime around 1767 on the Danish sugar island of St. Thomas, Telemaque was purchased by a Charleston-based slave trader, Captain Joseph Vesey. The fourteen-year-old cabin boy sailed the Atlantic with his new owner, eventually arriving in South Carolina, where, as a young man, he would join the newly formed African Methodist Episcopal Church. Vesey led classes and Bible study from his home and earned the reputation and honor of becoming one of Charleston's black preachers. He must have believed that it was the grace of God that brought him the most cherished blessing—his freedom.

In November of 1799, Denmark Vesey won fifteen hundred dollars in the city lottery, a blessing that would eventually set him free. Vesey immediately negotiated the terms of his freedom, purchasing himself for six hundred dollars on New Year's Eve. But while Vesey was blessed with his liberty, his wife remained enslaved—her owner refusing Vesey the ability to purchase her or his children. Vesey's happiness slowly evaporated, and the thirty-two-year-old carpenter realized that his freedom meant very little if his family remained enslaved. It was perhaps his faith that helped him endure the next twenty years, but eventually, Vesey began to preach from the Old Testament.

He declared that the enslaved were the chosen people—the New Israelites. Their God would punish all who participated in the fiendish institution of slavery, and he would lead the charge.

Vesey began to plan an insurrection. Free and enslaved blacks would rise up, kill their masters as they slept, steal guns from the city arsenal, and make their way to the docks with a plan to leave for Haiti. The attack would take place on July 14, 1822, a Sunday. But just like Gabriel Prosser's plan, it never happened. The plot was foiled, hundreds of black people were arrested, and panic spread throughout the city. Thirty-five people, including Vesey, were sentenced to death at the gallows. His church was destroyed, and once again white authorities tightened the slave codes in and around the state of South Carolina.

TO READ AND WRITE

In the North, however, a movement to end slavery was expanding. Northern blacks capitalized on new technologies in printing, using newspapers to fight the system of human bondage. The black press offered a safe space to galvanize support for the immediate abolition of slavery, and in the spring of 1827, free black abolitionists, such as Rev. Peter Williams, Jr., of New York published the first black-owned newspaper, *Freedom's Journal.* Williams offered reports about black rebellions, meetings, and anti-slavery activism, and began a long legacy of newspaper reporting by black men and women, Frederick Douglass and Mary Ann Shadd Cary among them.

Northern black revolutionaries and their allies organized themselves collectively and individually. Some participated in anti-slavery societies while others, such as David Walker, chose more radical actions. Born free in Wilmington, North Carolina, yet surrounded by enslaved people, Walker left his hometown and moved to Charleston, South Carolina. He lived through the aftermath of the Denmark Vesey plot and eventually headed north in search of opportunity. Walker settled in Boston, Massachusetts, where his hatred for slavery spilled onto the pages of what would become the most infamous anti-slavery pamphlet published in the United States. On September 28, 1829, Walker published an *Appeal . . . to the Colored Citizens of the World*, a radical seventy-six-page

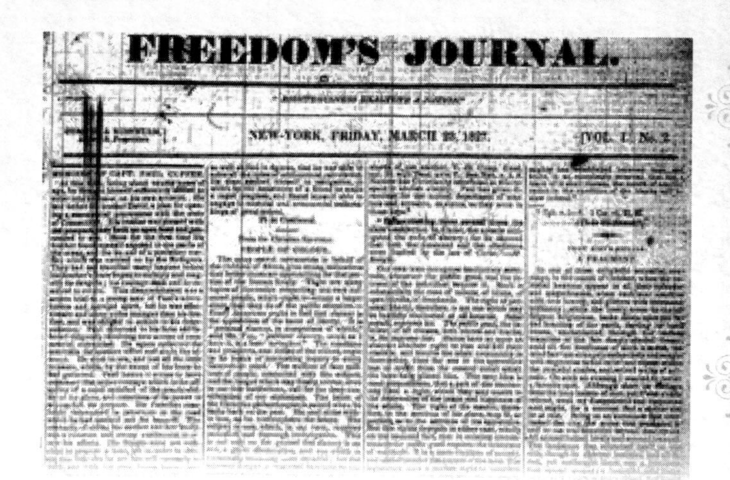

FREEDOM'S JOURNAL.

NEW-YORK, FRIDAY, MARCH

A New York African-American newspaper, edited by John B. Russwurm and Samuel Cornish.

pamphlet that challenged blacks worldwide to unify and combat whites in the fight to end slavery. Walker declared that whites were an "unjust, jealous, unmerciful, avaricious and blood-thirsty set of beings," who constantly "sought power and authority." The pamphleteer threw down the gauntlet, challenging the humanity of slave owners without fear of white retaliation.

Southern enslavers despised Walker and prohibited the sale and circulation of his work or any other "seditious" literature in their states. Georgia lawmakers placed a $10,000 bounty on Walker's head (equivalent to $262,000 today), but this did not stop him. He smuggled his call to action into the South by secretly sewing the *Appeal* into the lining of jackets worn by black sailors. Walker's life ended in 1830, when his dead body was found in his home. Many believed that Walker had been poisoned; however, more recent scholarship suggests that he died from tuberculosis.

Walker's life was cut short at the age of thirty-three, but committed abolitionists did not forget his words. His legacy prompted organizations such as the American Anti-Slavery Society to host rallies, publish newspapers, introduce legislation, aid runaways, and share their platforms with the world. Walker proved that the pen was powerful, but so too was the sword. The authority of his words was evident, threatening, and prophetic. He warned of a future leader of a great rebellion, and many believe this leader was Nat Turner.

TO PROPHESIZE

Perhaps it was his birth year that marked him: 1800 was a year filled with change, both turbulent and promising, when Americans watched slave owner Thomas Jefferson win a presidential election. His victory was later called the "revolution of 1800." For the enslaved, however, life became more vulnerable, perhaps more violent, as white farmers moved south and west to paint the countryside white with cotton. As the young nation celebrated a new president-elect, it did so with the recent memory of a foiled slave insurrection. Just a few months before the election, Gabriel Prosser was betrayed, destroying what could have been one of the most powerful and devastating examples of black resistance. But in the same year that Prosser's plot was exposed, two baby boys were born, one in Connecticut and another in Virginia. The New Englander would be named John Brown; the Southerner, Nat Turner.

Life was difficult on remote farms, and the enslaved were reminded of their bondage every time they came in contact with one of the seventeen hundred free blacks who lived in Southampton.

Born in October, the week before Gabriel Prosser was hanged, Nat grew up on the farm of Benjamin Turner in Southampton County, Virginia. Located just seventy miles south of Richmond, along the North Carolina border, Southampton counted a total population of a little over sixteen thousand people, and nearly half of them were enslaved. These men and women worked the fields to produce crops like corn, cotton, and tobacco, but the county was known for its bacon and its brandy. Life was difficult on remote farms, and the enslaved were reminded of their bondage every time they came in contact with one of the seventeen hundred free blacks who lived in Southampton. Very little is known about Nat's parents, except that he knew and lived with them. This is worth mentioning, as many children were torn from their parents at the earliest of ages, but Turner was among the fortunate in that he had the support and guidance of

Engraving depicting Nat Turner's Rebellion in Southampton County, Virginia.

parents and his grandmother. A nuclear family was the bedrock of Turner's formative years.

Oral tradition tells us that Nat Turner's mother arrived in Norfolk, Virginia, during the 1790s. Her owner, who fled from the slave revolt of Saint-Domingue, brought her to America, where she was eventually purchased by Benjamin Turner. Her name was Nancy. We have less in the way of records or folklore to describe Nat Turner's father, other than that he was supportive of his son, even under the most difficult of conditions. But his time with Nat Turner would be short-lived, for he made the desperate and risky decision to leave his family—he escaped. We do not know if Nat Turner's father made it to one of the free Northern states or if he perished along the way. However, he made an indelible impression on his son, perhaps teaching him that a release from slavery was worth any cost. No matter who was hurt in the process.

As a boy, Turner became known for his keen intelligence, learning to read at an early age, an act that earned him a reputation as gifted. His literacy was admired by everyone in his community and led him to a relationship with the Bible. Turner himself said that his faith was marked early by distinct growths that appeared on his head and chest. His deep belief in God and his religious practice would remain steadfast.

In 1809, Nat, his mother Nancy, and a handful of slaves were loaned out to Benjamin Turner's son, Samuel. This arrangement would become permanent the following year, after the death of the Turner family's patriarch. Old Bridget, Nat's grandmother, would remain at the old plantation, separated from her family until sometime before 1822. Nat Turner became a man on Samuel Turner's farm. He grew to about five feet seven inches tall, weighed close to 160 pounds, and would later be described as having "a bright complexion but not a mulatto." As he matured, his faith deepened, perhaps enough to make him believe that an escape from Southampton County was possible.

As a boy, Turner became known for his keen intelligence, learning to read at an early age, an act that earned him a reputation as gifted.

Some accounts suggest that in 1821 or 1822, Nat ran away from Samuel Turner's farm and remained at large for more than thirty days, eventually returning by his own volition. Perhaps his temporary escape had everything to do with a forced separation from his wife, a woman named Cherry. The couple endured what millions of other slaves experienced; they were sold away from each other.

Although the historical records around Nat Turner's wife are spotty at best, we know that she had lived at Samuel Turner's farm since 1807 and gave birth to at least one child, perhaps a son named Riddick. In 1822, Nat and his wife Cherry were torn apart when they were sold to new owners, a common family-fracturing event that often occurred when owners died or found themselves mired in debt. Cherry and her son were sold to Giles Reese. Nat Turner was sold to Thomas Moore for $400. The couple would have to carry on their relationship apart from each other.

Nat Turner's ownership would change hands again in 1830, following the death of Thomas Moore. He would become the property of Moore's young son Putnam, and would eventually be managed by the widow Moore's new husband, Joseph Travis, a wheelwright and carriage maker. Children often inherited enslaved people, but they

Nat and his wife Cherry were torn apart when they were sold to new owners, a common family-fracturing event that often occurred when owners died or found themselves mired in debt.

required an adult to supervise their human property. By 1831, Nat Turner had suffered under four separate owners, and had watched the devastation of slavery claim the lives of his family and friends. He looked to his Lord for an answer, and he received the Word.

As a child, Turner came to love God, the Bible, and the power of prayer. His faith was overpowering and prompted a self-baptism sometime around 1827. From this point forward, he relied on religious and spiritual gifts to survive enslavement, and like all enslaved people who believed in a higher power, Turner looked to his God for signs in times of trouble. His material possessions were few, but his Bible had to have been his most valued belonging. Many believe that he was always in communication with God and that Turner had an unusual command over the clouds. Turner paid close attention to what he believed were signs from God manifested in the natural world.

Shortly after his baptism, while working in the fields Turner saw drops of blood fall from the sky and land on the corn he held is his hands. To him, this was the blood of Christ returning to earth like early morning dew. It was his maker speaking to him, his God sharing the blood of life with him, and the spirit of the most high acknowledging his presence. Turner continued to look for God in everything.

When a solar eclipse occurred on February 12, 1831, Turner saw this event as a message from his Lord. This was no inexplicable vision; instead, it was an event documented by many almanacs, all of which acknowledged this exceptional occasion. There appeared in the sky a luminous ring around the sun, one that resembled a halo. It was at this moment that Turner knew his God had spoken. Six months later, on August 13, 1831, another solar eclipse turned the sun to a shade of bluish green. Turner believed it was his signal to act.

On Sunday, August 21, 1831, Nat Turner met with six enslaved comrades in the woods near Cabin Pond. His group of trusted rebels had expanded over the course of the spring and summer, but discretion remained a priority. This gathering was a final meeting and last meal before the fighting commenced. Hark brought a pig for roasting, and Henry Porter contributed a sample of the county's well-known brandy. Nelson Edwards, Sam, Will, and Jack arrived and waited. Nat Turner was the last of the men to join the group. They ate and they plotted. Turner drew a map of the county in pokeberry juice and strategically planned their revolt. They would kill all who owned slaves, beginning with the white men, women, and children who claimed the rebels as their personal property. Their attack began in the early morning hours of August 22, and it would be the Travis family, Nat Turner's enslavers, who would die first. Turner was armed with a hatchet, Hark had an axe, Will held a broadaxe, and the others armed themselves with other sharp tools that would carry out their mission.

By the middle of the day the rebels had grown in size, numbering nearly sixty insurgents. They had already killed people on eleven different farms. Turner and his growing militia believed that they were strong enough to attack Jerusalem, the county's seat, so they continued with their tour of duty. Eventually, the local militia would gather its might to suppress the rebellion. On the next day, a partial lunar eclipse signaled the end of Turner's revolt, and the capture and killing of most of the insurgents commenced. Nat Turner remained at large, not captured until October 30. Once he was handed over to local law enforcement, he was kept in isolation, but he was at peace and ready to meet his maker. Few people saw him, with the exception of guards and an attorney. His trial would be speedy.

He had been alone for nearly six weeks before his capture, while the community

After sixty-eight days in hiding, Nat Turner was captured by local farmer Benjamin Phipps.

around him was thrown into utter chaos. Throughout Virginia and North Carolina, blacks, enslaved and free, were beaten, murdered, and hung as a response to the rebellion. Turner's insurrection had been so bloody, so terrifying, that it prompted Virginians to rethink the institution of slavery. They wondered if white lives would be better protected if slavery were to cease. These questions would go unanswered because the state of Virginia had too much invested in the system of human bondage. Virginians would never agree to voluntarily turn over their property.

Much of what is known about the early life of Nat Turner descends from an important yet troublesome document. *The Confessions of Nat Turner* was published in November of 1831 by Thomas Gray, a thirty-one-year-old attorney who had access to Nat Turner as he awaited trial. In 1829, Gray was a fairly prosperous planter, owning twenty-one slaves on an eight-hundred-acre farm. But by 1831 his farm had been reduced in size by nearly 60 percent and he held only one remaining slave. After being cut out of his father's will, Gray was in desperate need of cash, and a publication based on the most sensationalized slave rebellion would most certainly end his financial calamity.

For many years, *The Confessions* was the central source used to study the rebellion in Southampton County, which is problematic. Confessionals must be read carefully, as they are often coerced, or even fabricated. No one knows exactly what was said between Gray and Turner as they talked in his jail cell, days before he was condemned to hang. Gray's supposed notes and the first draft of his manuscript are still missing to this day. The attorney-turned-writer did not hang around Southampton County long enough to witness Nat Turner's hanging. He was on his way to Baltimore, to meet with a publisher.

On November 6, Nat Turner took a short walk to the courthouse, where he calmly awaited his fate. The justice of the peace sentenced him to hang until he was "dead! dead! dead!" Nat Turner and his followers turned the system of slavery upside down, and in 1841, so too would Madison Washington and his comrades.

TO MUTINY

A ship named the *Creole* left Hampton Roads, Virginia, at midnight on October 17, 1841, carrying 135 enslaved people. Aboard the ship was Madison Washington, a fugitive who had once successfully escaped bondage by fleeing to Canada. But as with Denmark Vesey, his freedom meant nothing without his wife. Washington made the risky trip back to Virginia to collect her but was apprehended, taken to Richmond, and placed onto a ship that would deposit him at a New Orleans slave market. The former fugitive conspired with fellow shipmates Ben Blacksmith and Elijah Morris, and on November 7, 1841, the human cargo overpowered the ship's crew, stabbed a slave trader to death, and steered the vessel to the Bahamas. They knew that the island was free territory, as the British had abolished slavery there in the1830s. The mutineers were greeted by black Bahamians, who eventually boarded the ship and declared that the passengers were free. Nineteen of the mutineers were temporarily imprisoned while U.S. agents argued that all of the enslaved cargo should be returned to New Orleans. This would never happen. All the mutineers were released from prison, and along with most of their other shipmates, they made new lives for themselves in the Bahamas and Jamaica.

Enraged over their loss of property, a handful of enslavers filed claims with insurance companies and used the courts to sue for compensation. Some of the cases were heard by the Louisiana Supreme Court, however the majority were dismissed. Insurance policies were canceled under certain circumstances, particularly if an enslaved person committed suicide or participated in a rebellion or conspiracy. Nearly ten years later, the Anglo-American Claims Commission paid the United States $110,000 for the loss of enslaved property. Today, that same claim would be worth $3.5 million dollars.

TO ESCAPE

Slave owners were always willing to spend a little money to make a lot of money. When enslaved men and women made the decision to take a chance and run for freedom, slave owners often placed paid advertisements in local newspapers. Financial rewards proved a successful incentive as slave catchers roamed the cities of the urban North looking for human property. Handsome payouts were likely if slaves were returned healthy and relatively unharmed. This was the case for Lear Green, who in the fall of 1850 had a $150 bounty placed on her head.

The Maryland woman fled from her owner so that she could marry her love, William Adams, a free black barber. Adams had proposed to her, but Green hesitated, knowing all too well that their marriage would never be legally recognized because she remained enslaved. Any children that came from their union would add to her owner's wealth, as their enslaved status would be inherited from their mother. These future children could be sold away at a moment's notice, and Green would not begin her family under these circumstances. She accepted his proposal and thought of ways to guarantee marriage in a free state.

Her escape was carefully planned as she prepared to ship herself to freedom. She climbed into a box, smaller than a coffin, and prepared for the dangerous voyage ahead. With the help of Adams's mother, Green entered a sailor's chest about the size of the overhead compartment on a contemporary airplane. She equipped herself with a quilt,

1 October 2, 1800:

An enslaved African woman named Nancy Turner gave birth to Nat Turner on a plantation in Southampton County, Virginia.

As a child, Nat Turner was said to be prophetic, and was taught how to read and write, and studied religion.

2 Unknown Date, 1810–1811:

Nat's father escapes from the Turner plantation.

3 Unknown Date, 1821/22:

Turner marries an enslaved woman named Cherry.

4 Unknown Date, 1822–1825:

Turner begins preaching and experiencing religious visions.

He soon becomes known as "the slave preacher."

Anti-Slavery Revolts

1712–1841

Cato's Conspiracy
1739

A group of approximately 23 enslaved blacks planned and executed an attack on slavery in New York. They used swords, knives, hatchets, guns, and arson to kill at least nine white slave owners, and injured another six.

Afterward, 27 conspirators were captured and of these, 6 committed suicide, 21 were convicted and publicly executed by being burned at the stake or hanged by chains. This rebellion resulted in stricter laws forbidding blacks from congregating and holding firearms.

The Stono Rebellion *occurred on Sunday, September 9, 1739, in South Carolina. Led by an enslaved African named Jemmy, who directed a la group of enslaved Africans, including 20 from the Kingdom of Kongo, execute the largest slave uprising in the British mainland colonies.*

The rebels sang and drummed to signal their movement and gathered upward of 100 supporters, and killed approximately 25 whites. When th rebellion was stopped, roughly 44 blacks were killed on the spot and th who remained were eventually captured and executed. This revolt led to the 1740 Negro Act, which prohibited blacks from growing their own fo congregating, working for pay, and gaining literacy.

The Insurrection of 1741 *was a suspected conspiracy, which by harsh economic and social conditions and the paranoia fr of uprisings during the 1730s. Ten fires were set throughout which were attributed to slaves and poor whites. 152 free an blacks were arrested in connection with this plot; 30 were ex majority of the others were sold to the Caribbean.*

1

April 6, 1712
New York Slave Rebellion
(New York)

2

September 9, 1739
Stono Rebellion
(South Carolina)

3

March–April 1741
New York Slave Insurrection of 1741

4

1791–
The

9

10

October 30, 1831:

After 68 days in hiding, Turner is captured.

He is held in the county jail, where he purportedly makes his "confessions" to lawyer Thomas Gray.

November 5, 1831:

Turner is tried for insurrection, found guilty, and sentenced to death.

November 11, 1831:

Nat Turner is hanged before a multitude of spectators. Following execution it is believed that Turner's body is beheaded and skinned, his flesh churned into grease.

Winter 1832—Following the Turner rebellion, the Virginia Legislature considered abolishing slavery. Some legislators desired full emancipation; others argued for heightened restrictions and the removal of all free blacks from the state. In a close vote, the legislature decided to continue slavery. Consequently, the legislature passed laws banning the teaching of reading and writing to all blacks, regardless of their status. Blacks were now forbidden to preach, to travel, to attend or conduct church in the absence of an overseer or an appointed white, to carry firearms, and purchase a slave who was not one's husband, wife, or child.

The Haitian Revolution *was a successful antislavery and anticolonial insurrection that took place in the French colony of Saint-Domingue, which lasted from 1791 until 1804.*

The revolution resulted in the liberation of the enslaved population and the expulsion of the French, and made Haiti the first free black nation in the Western Hemisphere. It impacted the institution of slavery throughout the slave-holding colonies and is considered a major turning point in antislavery thought.

An enslaved blacksmith, ***Gabriel Prosser,*** *organized a plot to attack Richmond. The plans for the revolt were leaked prior to its execution, and he and 25 followers were taken captive and hanged.*

This plot resulted in the refinement of Virginia's slave laws; deportation as an alternative to capital punishment, abolition of private manumissions, and mandatory deportation of free blacks. In the end, 72 men were tried, and 26 were found guilty and hanged, 8 were transported, 13 declared guilty, but pardoned by the governor due to economic reasons, and 25 were acquitted.

ge
e
se
od,

was fueled
m the series
ew York City,
enslaved
cuted, and the

During the harvest season in 1811, Haitian-born slave driver ***Charles Deslondes*** *led close to 500 slaves, armed with guns, pikes, hoes, and axes, who carried banners and marched to the beat of drums while chanting "Freedom or Death" along the east bank of the Mississippi River, in what is now the St. John the Baptist and St. Charles Parishes.*

66 rebels were killed during the fighting, 17 went missing, and 18 were arrested, convicted, executed and their heads were removed and put on stakes along the Mississippi River. Deslondes was executed, mutilated, and put on public display. While this was the largest slave revolt in American history, only two white men were killed.

5

6

1804
Haitian Revolution

August 30, 1800
Gabriel's Conspiracy
(Henrico County, VA)

January 8–9, 1811
German Coast Slave Uprising
(Louisiana)

5

6

7

8

February 12, 1831:

Nat believed that a solar eclipse was a sign to revolt. He begins holding secret meetings with fellow slaves to outline the strategy for a revolution.

August 21, 1831:

In the afternoon Turner and his rebels met at Cabin Pond and by the middle of the night they started the revolt at the Travis Farm.

Turner and the rebels travel from house to house, killing slave-owning family members by knife, ax, and club.

August 23, 1831:

The slave rebellion marches toward the armory in nearby Jerusalem, where they are confronted by a large militia, including state and federal troops. Though Turner escapes, dozens of slaves are captured and hanged without trial.

Fall 1831:

Brutal reprisals begin, with hundreds of innocent enslaved free blacks indiscriminately ki in retribution.

Severed heads are displayed a posts throughout the county ar surrounding region to promote fear among enslaved populati

Nat Turner's Rebellion *took place in Southampton County, Virginia, during August 1831. Nat Turner's army killed between 55 to 65 people, the highest number of white fatalities caused by any slave uprising in the United States.*

The rebellion was quelled within a few days, but Turner survived in hiding for more than two months afterward. Turner and his rebels were tried, convicted, and executed; their heads were put on posts, and it is said that Turner's headless body was skinned, boiled, and turned into souvenirs.

In the aftermath, whites tortured and terrorized innocent blacks as a way to suppress further rebellion.

During the height of the U.S. domestic slave trade, a ship carrying 135 enslaved people from Richmond to New Orleans was overthrown by the captives. The revolt was led by an enslaved man named Madison Washington, who had recently learned details about the Amistad case.

The 18 rebels killed a slave trader, wounded the captain, seized control of the ship, and steered it to nearby Nassau, ultimately liberating 130 enslaved African-Americans and deeming it the most successful slave revolt in U.S. history.

AMOSKEAG CANAL LOTTERY—NO. 2. FIRST CLASS. No.

THIS Ticket ſhall entitle the bearer to receive the prize that may be drawn againſt its number, agreeably to an Act of the General Court of New Hampſhire, paſſed June 17th, 1802, if demanded within ſix months.

Denmark Vesey *(also named Telemaque) was born on the Danish island of St. Thomas and was sold to Charleston at the age of 14. He was a literate, skilled carpenter, and a preacher at the African Methodist Church in Charleston. At the age of 32, he won a lottery, and purchased his own freedom.*

In his mid-50s, Vesey planned a revolution, where enslaved blacks would kill their masters and escape to Haiti. His plan was leaked before it was enacted, and as a result 35 blacks were hanged at the gallows.

The Amistad Revolt *took place on board the Spanish schooner* La Amistad, *which was carrying 53 Mende captives from Sierra Leone. A 25-year old Sengbe Pieh (Cinque) led the fight, which took control of the ship. The rebels successfully overthrew the crew and demanded a return to West Africa. The navigators intentionally took them to Long Island, NY, in an attempt to keep them in bondage. The rebels were jailed for 18 months, and stood trial, and the 35 survivors were eventually set free and returned to their native land.*

7

June–July 1822 Denmark Vesey Conspiracy of 1822
(Charleston, South Carolina)

8

August 21–23, 1831
Nat Turner's Rebellion
(Southampton County, VA)

9

July 1–August 24, 1839
The Amistad Revolt
(The coast of Long Island, NY)

10

November 7, 1841
The Creole Revolt
(Eastern Shore of the United States)

a pillow, and a few articles of clothing, perhaps to protect her from a bumpy journey. She had only a small amount of food and a bottle of water to sustain her aboard a steamship from Baltimore to Philadelphia.

Her soon to be mother-in-law traveled with the chest, checking on Green in the middle of the night to make certain that she was still alive. She lifted the lid on the chest to allow for fresh air, an act that allowed Green to survive her harrowing voyage.

After an eighteen-hour journey, a stagecoach delivered the sailor's chest to the office of black abolitionist William Still. A famed conductor of the Underground Railroad, Still described Green as a "dark-brown color," with a "countenance . . . of peculiar modesty and grace." Still was one of many black abolitionists who placed their lives in danger to help fugitives such as Green, a task that became more and more difficult as the1850s progressed. In the end Lear Green and William Adams married and settled in Elmira, New York.

TO SURVIVE

In the years leading up to the Civil War, America moved at lightning speed into two different orbits. Southerners clung to slavery while Northerners divested themselves of it, creating a thick tension that would erupt in violence and bloodshed. But on October 16 and 17 of 1859, a Connecticut-born tanner by the name of John Brown led a small interracial group of followers to attack the institution of slavery. The mission was simple and their objective mighty, as followers planned to raid the federal arsenal in Virginia (today West Virginia), steal weapons, and start an uprising in hopes of abolishing slavery. It was a two-day war and only one survivor lived to tell about the raid on Harper's Ferry. Osborne P. Anderson, a free black man, managed to avoid death via battle or the gallows. He fled from the bloody scene, venturing on a five-hundred-mile journey to Canada. Osborne Anderson's *A Voice from Harper's Ferry* offered America a firsthand account of all that transpired at the most infamous attack on slavery's grip. It would mark the survival of a people and a legacy of resistance that continues today.

Blacks, enslaved and free, resisted oppression by asserting themselves as human beings with rights. Nat Turner used multiple forms of resistance to free himself from slavery. He organized, he plotted, he marched, he preached, he read, and he mutinied against the oppressive system. Others, like those in New York, set fire to their farms and homesteads or shipped themselves to freedom, while some survived by escaping to free territory in Canada, the Bahamas, or other parts of the world. We know that their brave acts of liberty occurred on a daily basis and sometimes created a path of destruction that led to the brutal deaths of enslavers of all ages. About this, Turner allegedly believed that "nits make lice" and that no lives should be spared. He was not alone in his thinking. However, it is for us to decide what slaves thought on the eve of rebellious events. Did they understand the magnitude of their actions? Or were they simply trying to survive? History tells us that their courage and tenacity were evident.

This time, he took a deep breath, calmly exhaled, and said, "I'm ready."

Nat Turner never had the opportunity to say good-bye to his family. Never again would he lay eyes upon his wife, Cherry, or his progeny. Instead, he prepared himself to meet his God. Most prisoners were given a last meal prior to execution, but Nat Turner's Last Supper was with friends, in the woods at Cabin Pond nearly twelve weeks earlier.

On a chilly winter morning in Jerusalem, Virginia, Nat Turner was escorted to the gallows. We do not know what he was thinking, but it is likely that he focused on God and the scriptures that had sustained him for thirty-one years. Those who came to witness his death jeered at him as he calmly took his place on the platform. They were angry because Turner and his followers had stood up to a brutal system and confirmed slave owners' greatest fears. Enslaved people rebelled. As a result, legislation throughout the North and South placed greater restrictions on blacks (enslaved and free). But on this day, November 11, 1831, a community stood still. It was Nat Turner's last day on earth. Soon he would join his ancestors in a higher spiritual place. Turner knew God and had been preaching the gospel for most of his life. Perhaps he turned to Him, and looked up at the sky as he had done on so many occasions. This time, he took a deep breath, calmly exhaled, and said, "I'm ready." After he'd been hung, he was decapitated, and folklore tells us that his body parts were made into souvenirs. He never received a proper burial. But today, the spirit of Nat Turner lives in *The Birth of a Nation*.

NOTE

We have chosen to use the word "slave" throughout the text of this essay for the purpose of narrative flow. As scholars, we prefer to use the term "enslaved" when referring to men and women who were held in bondage. The word "enslaved" shifts the attention to the action that was placed upon the bodies of black people. It is a term that reinforces their status as human property (chattel).

SOURCES

Akinyela, Makungu M. "Battling the Serpent: Nat Turner, Africanized Christianity, and the Black Ethos." *Journal of Black Studies* 33, No. 3 (January 2003): 255–280.

Allmendinger, David. *Nat Turner and the Rising in Southampton County* (Baltimore: Johns Hopkins University Press, 2014).

Aptheker, Herbert. *American Negro Slave Revolts* (1943. Reprint. New York: International Publishers, 1983).

Breen, Patrick. *The Land Shall Be Deluged in Blood: A New History of the Nat Turner Revolt* (New York: Oxford University Press, 2016).

Brown, William Wells. *Clotel & Other Writings* (New York: Library of America, 2014).

Carroll, Joseph Cephas. *Slave Insurrections in the United States, 1800–1865* (New York: Dover Publications, 2004).

Egerton, Doug. *Gabriel's Rebellion: The Virginia Slave Conspiracies of 1800 and 1802* (Chapel Hill: University of North Carolina Press, 1993).

Egerton, Doug. *He Shall Go Out Free: The Lives of Denmark Vesey* (Lanham, MD: Rowman & Littlefield Publishers, 2004).

Forrest, William S. *Historical and Descriptive Sketches of Norfolk and Vicinity: Including Portsmouth and the Adjacent Counties, During a Period of Two Hundred Years; Also Sketches of Williamsburg, Hampton, Suffolk, Smithfield, and Other Places, with Descriptions of Some of the Principal Objects of Interest in Eastern Virginia* (Philadelphia: Lindsay and Blakiston, 1853).

Franklin, John Hope, and Evelyn Higginbotham. *From Slavery to Freedom: A History of African Americans* (New York: McGraw Hill, 2011).

Greenberg, Kenneth, ed. *Nat Turner in History and Memory* (New York: Oxford University Press, 2003).

Hinks, Peter P. *To Awaken My Afflicted Brethren: David Walker and the Problem of Antebellum Slave Resistance* (University Park: Pennsylvania State University Press, 1997).

Lepore, Jill. *New York Burning: Liberty, Slavery, and Conspiracy in Eighteenth-Century Manhattan* (New York: Vintage Books, 2005).

Rawick, George. *From Sundown to Sunup: The Making of the Black Community* (Westport, CT: Greenwood, 1972).

Santoro, Anthony. "The Prophet in His Own Words: Nat Turner's Biblical Construction." *Virginia Magazine of History and Biography* 116, No. 2 (2008): 114–149.

Still, William. *The Underground Railroad: A Record of Facts, Authentic Narrative, Letters, &C.* (Philadelphia: Porter & Coates, 1972).

Walker, David. *Appeal, in Four Articles; Together with a Preamble, to the Coloured Citizens of the World, but in Particular, and Very Expressly, to Those of the United States of America*, 3rd ed. (Boston: published by the author, 1830).

Wood, Peter. *Black Majority: Negroes in Colonial South Carolina From 1670 Through the Stono Rebellion* (New York: W.W. Norton, 1974).

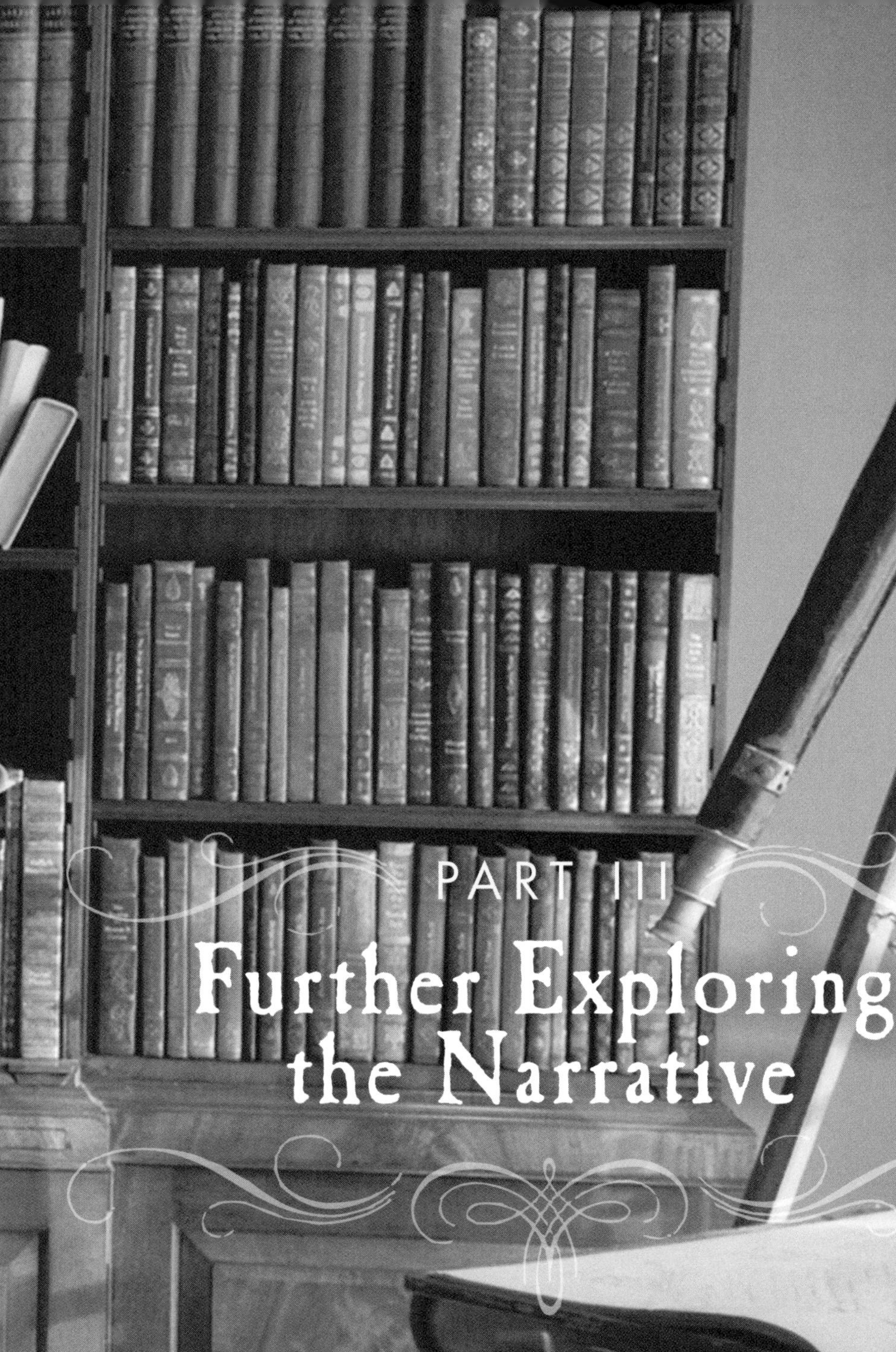

PART III

Further Exploring the Narrative

BLACKHEAD SIGNPOST RD
658

Slavery and (In)Justice During the Nat Turner Rebellion:

History and Legacy of the "Rule of Law" in America

BY *ALFRED* L. *BROPHY*

The United States Supreme Court's 1954 opinion in *Brown v. Board of Education* left us with the belief that courts are the place to go for "justice." There is something grand about Americans' optimism that courts are designed to adjudicate cases fairly. Yet, as the Black Lives Matter movement has recently reminded us, the reality of the legal system is different from our nation's vision of fairness and justice. For we have recently seen the criminal justice system fail many of our nation's African-American citizens—and other citizens, too. The gap between the *vision* of "law" as justice and the *reality* of law is rather large; many are left behind by law's promise.

This was particularly true in the era of slavery. As the Nat Turner rebellion highlights, in the years before the Civil War, slave law was primarily an instrument that helped the white slave society maintain control over the enslaved population. And therein lies an important story about why Turner had to turn to violence if he were to take effective action against slavery. The legal system did not allow slaves to take much action. It largely excluded them from court and from the ballot box. The laws of Virginia set up a system of slave patrols to make sure that slaves were kept in their place, limited the ability to teach slaves to read, prevented owners from freeing slaves in many circumstances, and required those who were freed to leave the state or face re-enslavement. In short, the law enforced black slavery and white supremacy and drastically limited rights of enslaved people.

In 1830, the year before the Turner rebellion, a North Carolina Supreme Court justice overturned the conviction of a white man who shot an enslaved woman who was running away from him. The court protected the rights of slaveholders (in this case a white man who had rented this woman) to shoot slaves. "We cannot allow the right of the master to be brought into discussion in the courts of justice," wrote the judge. To maintain slavery, the slave "must be made sensible that there is no appeal from his master."[1] And that is how the legal system operated in the slave-owning South. The enslaved were objects of control and producers of wealth, who were required to obey their owners or face punishment at the hands of the owners—or the state. When a slave owner and his family were killed in 1852 by two slaves, a Richmond, Virginia, minister told an African-American congregation that they had to be even more meek than they had been before, or they would face terrible violence:

> In your respective spheres of life you will have to be more obedient and submissive for the future than you have ever been heretofore, or else you will bring upon yourselves serious troubles. God has given this country to the white people. They are the law-makers . . . [and] the superiors. The people of color are the subjects—the servants—and even when not in bondage, the inferiors. In this state of things, God enjoins on you submission.[2]

There were, to be sure, a few instances where judges allowed slaves who claimed they should be free to sue for freedom; but those are a small handful of cases among the millions of people held in bondage. And over time the courts cut back even on those opportunities.[3]

---

1 *State v. Mann,* 13 N.C. (2 Dev.) 263, 267 (1830).

2 Robert Ryland, "Substance of a Sermon," in *Particulars of the Dreadful Tragedy in Richmond, on the Morning of the 19th July, 1852: Being a Full Account of the Awful Murder of the Winston Family* (Richmond, VA: John D. Hammersley, 1852), 36.

3 See, e.g., Lea Vandervelde, *Redemption Songs: Suing for Freedom Before Dred Scott* (New York: Oxford University Press, 2014).

Such was the world of law that Nat Turner inhabited. The legal system treated him as property and offered him no opportunity for freedom. Religion offered some sense of freedom; and he served as a minister for both black and white Virginians. But in the eyes of the law, Turner was property. He had been owned by several people—first by Benjamin Turner, who owned Nat's mother when he was born. When Turner died in 1810, he was inherited by Benjamin's son, Samuel, and when Samuel died in 1822, Turner was sold to Thomas Moore. In 1828, Thomas died and Turner became the property of Moore's young son, Putnam. Through the twists of inheritance law, Nat Turner became the property of a child. Religious ideas may have given Nat Tuner some inspiration for thinking that he could take action. He said in the *Confessions* that the Spirit told him in 1828 that "the time was fast approaching when the first should be last and the last should be first."[4] When asked after his capture whether he now realized he was mistaken, Turner responded, "Was not Christ crucified?"[5]

And crucified the Turner rebels and many others in the African-American community were. Violence was a core part of the response to the rebellion. One white man from North Carolina who was familiar with the aftermath of the rebellion wrote that

> they burnt off the foot of a negro whom they had taken into [custody] on suspicion & found at last that he was innocent. They had one of the ears cut off of another (who [was] . . . guilty of murdering his master in a most barbarous manner) & after rubbing the wound with sand, they tied him on a horse, had the horse mounted and rode, & then turned loose into the woods. Certainly this negro deserved to be punished in the most severe manner warranted by civilized society, but this Indian like treatment casts a great reflection on the troops by whom it was authorized.[6]

The stories of the extralegal executions are horrific. For instance, as the rebellion was still going on one rebel, perhaps a blacksmith named Alfred, was caught by the local militia. They did not have the time or means to take him into custody, so they cut the tendons in his feet so that he could not escape, then left him tied to a tree. Shortly afterward a mounted militia unit from a neighboring county, the Greensville Dragoons, happened upon Alfred and shot him, then placed his head on a pole. When Alfred's owner petitioned the Virginia legislature to ask for compensation for him, he surmised that the Southampton militia had killed him rather than holding him for trial because they "deemed that his immediate execution would operate as a beneficial example to the other insurgents—many of whom were still in arms and unsubdued."[7]

---

4 Thomas R. Gray, *The Confessions of Nat Turner: The Leader of the Late Insurrection in Southampton, Va.* (Baltimore: Lucas & Deaver, 1831), 11.

5 Ibid.

6 Letter from George W. Mordecai to Rachel Mordecai Lazarus (September 1831) (on file with the Wilson Library, University of North Carolina at Chapel Hill, in the George W. Mordecai Papers, #522).

7 Petition of Levi Waller, to the Gen. Assembly of Va., County of Southampton (circa 1831) (Library of Virginia, Southampton County, Petitions to the Legislature, Reel 184, Box 234). See also Alfred L. Brophy, "The Nat Turner Trials," *North Carolina Law Review* 91 (2013): 1817, 1832.

The echoes of Alfred's summary execution sound down to the present. The road where Alfred's head was placed is now called "Blackhead Signpost Road," though there is a movement afoot in Southampton to change it.[8]

Alfred's owner did not, however, receive compensation; nor did any of the other owners of slaves who were killed without trial. These were losses borne by individual slave owners, which is one reason why the extralegal violence was so dangerous, even to the white community. Leaders of the state tried to control the vigilante violence. General Richard Eppes, the head of the militia sent to put down the rebellion, pleaded for an end to the violence. "Acts of barbarity and cruelty," he admonished, "are never looked upon but with horror by any but savages."[9] While the legal system released owners from

The vigilante violence threatened to tear apart the entire community; no one's property or person would be safe.

liability for most of the violence against their human property—owners who killed their slaves were sometimes prosecuted—Eppes and other whites realized there had to be some controls on vigilante violence. This was partly because the vigilante violence against suspected rebels cost their owners their human property. Moreover, the vigilante violence threatened to tear apart the entire community; no one's property or person would be safe. North Carolina Supreme Court Justice William Gaston gave voice to these fears when he spoke to Princeton University students in 1835. Gaston asked for an end to violence against free black people and Catholics. If the law was not respected, neither people nor property would be safe, Gaston warned.[10]

---

8 Andrew Lind, "Road Name Change Proposed," *Tidewater News*, June 16, 2015 (discussing proposal of John Ricks, a retired Marine, to rename Blackhead Signpost Road).

9 "Domestic Tranquility Restored," *Richmond Enquirer*, September 6, 1831, 2.

10 William Gaston, *An Address Delivered Before the American Whig and Cliosophic Societies of the College of New Jersey* (Princeton, NJ: R. E. Hornor, 1835), 27.

Yet others believed the violence had served the important purpose of stopping more rebellions. The rebellion served as a warning to the white community to be more vigilant and less humane toward slaves, thought one white man. And it also served to remind the enslaved communities that they should not attempt rebellion. The slaves, he thought, "must be now satisfied that though they may succeed in doing much private injury in particular neighborhoods, yet they can never succeed to any extent, & they may therefore be induced to submit quietly to the evils of their unfortunate condition."[11]

After the immediate threat of the rebellion was put down and the vigilante violence was under control, there followed trials of more than forty suspected rebels in Southampton County and more than a dozen in nearby counties. Those trials attempted to sort out the most guilty—and then punished them with either death or sale outside the state. Twenty-one were charged with outright insurrection or murder; another twenty-two were charged with a less serious offense of conspiracy with the rebels. All but three of those charged with insurrection or murder were convicted, and most of them were executed. Nearly half of those tried for conspiracy were acquitted. In the neighboring county of Sussex another dozen slaves were tried. Even though the rebellion never reached Sussex, the fear of rebellion led to eight convictions. It seems the heat of passion swept up the court and the prosecutor.

But while much of the white community was resorting to violence—and the legal system—to restore order and slavery, some in the white community dissented from this. Prominent among them were lawyers for the rebels. One young lawyer, James Strange French, seems to have been interested in establishing some rudimentary fairness for slaves. French later wrote a novel that depicted Native Americans sympathetically.[12]

In the wake of the rebellion many white people asked what had motivated Turner. While Turner said he was motivated by religious ideas, some slave owners were concerned less with questions of his motivations and more with the lack of vigilance by Turner's owners and other slave owners in Southampton. One white woman in

---

11 Letter from George Mordecai to My Dear Father (September 2, 1831) (Wilson Library, University of North Carolina at Chapel Hill, in the Mordecai Family Papers, Series 1.2.1, Box 4, Folder 56), 2–3.

12 James Strange French, *Elkswatawa; Or, the Prophet of the West: A Tale of the Frontier* (New York: Harper & Bros., 1836).

Wilmington, North Carolina, stated that she knew not "whether to ascribe" the rebellion "to the evil inherent in man, or the powerful influence [of] that noble principle the love of freedom."[13] That was an important line of questioning: was Turner a violent and possibly insane killer or a freedom fighter? This question still looms large in Turner's legacy. The answer turned in part on how people thought about the requirement that slaves obey the rules of the slave society.

People at the time thought that the abolitionist literature was prompting the slaves to rebel. In the wake of the Nat Turner rebellion, Virginia's governor collected some recent radical pamphlets in circulation in Virginia, including David Walker's *Appeal to the Coloured Citizens of the World*, William Lloyd Garrison's *Address Delivered Before the Free People of Color in Philadelphia, New York, and Other Cities*, Charles Stuart's *Remarks on the Colony of Liberia and the American Colonization Society*, and Shadrack Bassett's *African Hymn*.[14] That abolitionist literature was blamed for setting in motion the actions of Turner and his fellow rebels. There was a sense that slaves were learning ideas of freedom from abolitionists, that the rebels were motivated not just by vengeance, but by anti-slavery ideas. That combination of impulses toward freedom and ideas of freedom struck fear in the minds of slave owners. In the wake of the rebellion, many wanted to fasten shackles even more tightly on slaves and to make it harder for them to hear the voices of abolitionist literature.

Two decades later Henry David Thoreau questioned the duty to uphold the law in the wake of the Fugitive Slave Act in his famous essay that we call "Civil Disobedience."[15] Thoreau was responding to those who were saying in churches, in the halls of Congress, and even at universities that it was the duty of United States citizens to uphold the Fugitive Slave Act and return fugitives in Northern states to slavery in Southern states. They argued in essence that the laws—whatever they were—had to be followed. But Thoreau and many others were guided by a different moral compass

---

13 Letter from Rachel Lazarus to My Dear Friend [Maria Edgeworth] (September 29, 1831) (on file with the Wilson Library, University of North Carolina at Chapel Hill, in the Mordecai Family Papers, Box 10, Folder 126).

14 John Floyd Letterbook (Library of Virginia, Reel 5391).

15 Henry David Thoreau, "Civil Disobedience," in *The Writings of Henry David Thoreau: Miscellanies* (Boston: Houghton, Mifflin, 1893), 131.

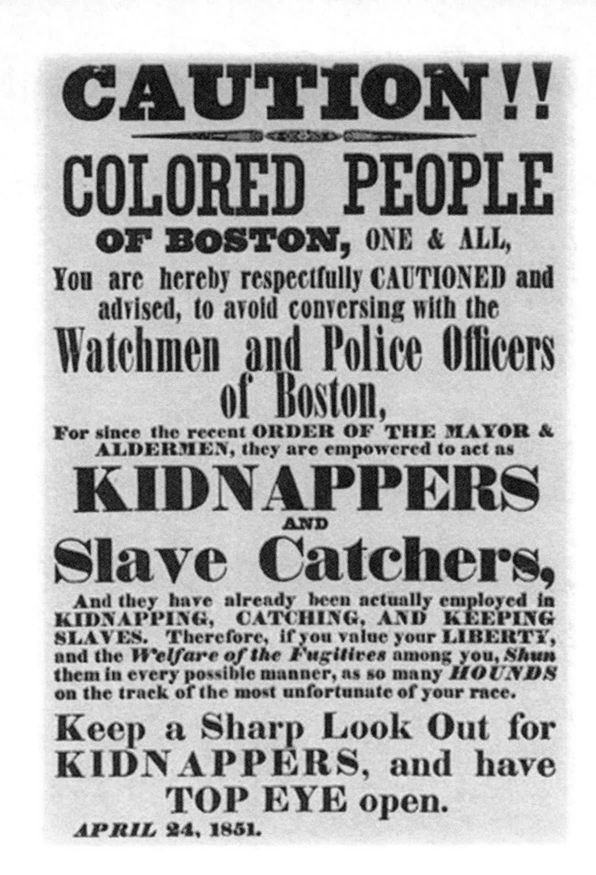
CAUTION!!

COLORED PEOPLE

OF BOSTON, ONE & ALL,

You are hereby respectfully CAUTIONED and advised, to avoid conversing with the

Watchmen and Police Officers of Boston,

For since the recent ORDER OF THE MAYOR & ALDERMEN, they are empowered to act as

KIDNAPPERS

AND

Slave Catchers,

And they have already been actually employed in KIDNAPPING, CATCHING, AND KEEPING SLAVES. Therefore, if you value your LIBERTY, and the *Welfare of the Fugitives* among you, *Shun* them in every possible manner, as so many *HOUNDS* on the track of the most unfortunate of your race.

Keep a Sharp Look Out for KIDNAPPERS, and have TOP EYE open.

APRIL 24, 1851.

A broadside used to warn African-Americans about slave catchers in Boston.

than the law of slave states and the United States government. This led to a vibrant and heated debate about whether citizens needed to follow the state and federal law of slavery—or whether they could follow something else, like their conscience about slavery. This was often known as a "higher law." Some, like Thoreau, made this an abstract question of justice versus law. Others followed in the footsteps of Nat Turner and the other rebels who had put ideas of freedom into action.

Whether Turner was a lawbreaker or a freedom fighter is a question we can—and should—debate. We are much better able than the slave owners in the 1830s to see why he might have chosen a path of violence. But even then people understood that when there was so little chance for freedom, and so much violence in the system of slavery, slaves might take to violence to free themselves. There were two very different interpretations, in which some abolitionists saw rebellion as right, while many other people, particularly slave owners, saw rebellion as an egregious violation of law.

It seems clear that Turner struck a blow for freedom the way he thought best. In the short term that led to tougher controls over blacks. However, in the long run his actions led others to challenge slavery, and that may have helped push the nation toward the Civil War that so quickly led to slavery's demise. The corollary to Victor Hugo's principle that "there is nothing so powerful as an idea whose time has come" is "there is nothing so powerless as an idea whose time has passed." Perhaps Turner helped lead the country to the realization that slavery's time had passed, because of the brutality that slavery fostered in the slaves and in the slave

Perhaps Turner helped lead the country to the realization that slavery's time had passed, because of the brutality that slavery fostered in the slaves and in the slave owners, too.

owners, too. Even though slavery was lawful in the 1830s and those who challenged it faced death, its days were already drawing to a rapid close. And the goal of "law" was being changed from the idea of slavery and control to one of freedom.

The struggle for equal treatment under law continues, as the Black Lives Matter movement has so powerfully reminded us. Though the means and issues for activism are radically different from the era when so many people struggled to bring down slavery, there are many who are seeking to bring attention to racial injustice in the legal system. The echoes of Turner's struggle against slavery appear in many places, from Southampton, where "Blackhead Signpost Road" reminds us of the extraordinary violence that once was used there to maintain people in slavery, to Hollywood, where artists seek to bring attention to the past and its parallels to the present.

ABOVE
Nat Turner's grandmother, played by Esther Scott, attending to his wounds.

RIGHT
Image of Gordon, an enslaved man who escaped from a Louisiana plantation.

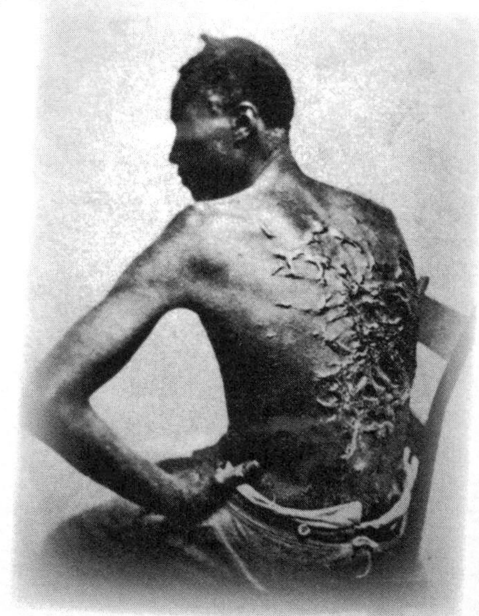

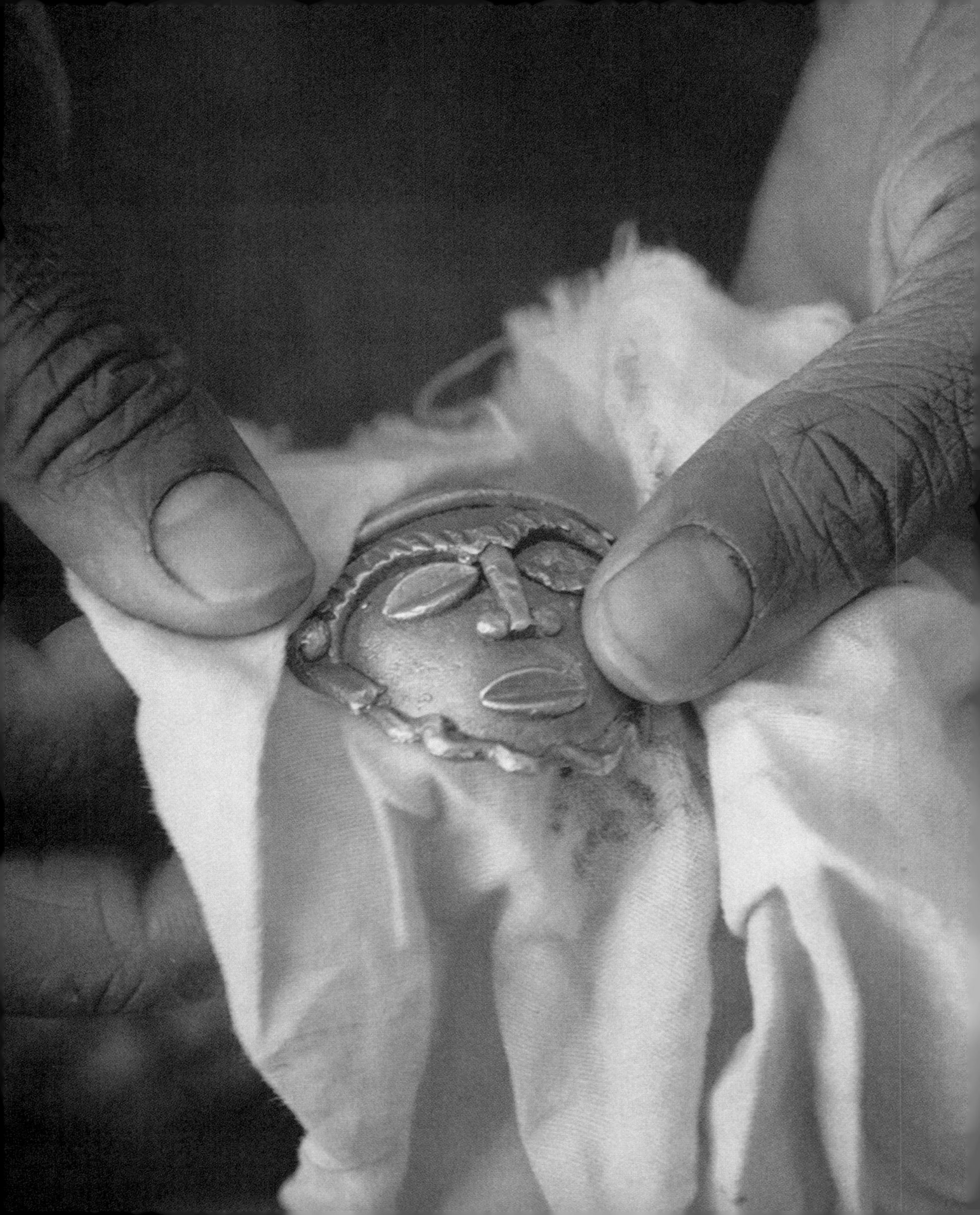

Nat Turner at the Crossroads: *African Iconography and Cosmologies in* The Birth of a Nation

BY KELLEY FANTO DEETZ

Some called her Old Bridget; as a child she survived a kidnapping in her native land of present-day Ghana, and she spent her adult life enslaved in Southampton County, Virginia. Her presumed Akan ethnicity undoubtedly marked her as a possible threat on the slave ship that carried her to the shores of America. Her daughter-in-law, Nancy, was also stolen from West Africa and eventually sold onto a Virginia plantation. Once on the ships that brought these women to Virginia soil, they witnessed and/or endured abuse, rape, and humiliation. Their world, and particularly their legacies, were reset by the traders who caught, traded, and sold them to the Virginia planters who held them in bondage until their deaths. Nancy and Bridget's societal positions in West Africa are unknown, but their connection and exposure to one of the most notorious ethnic groups in the Atlantic world speak volumes to their legacies. By the eighteenth century, slave traders understood the risks associated with some of their captives. Many West Africans and especially the Akan were notorious warriors, knowwn for their sophisticated and tactical styles. West African kingdoms were at war when the Portuguese made contact and started the transatlantic slave trade in the late fifteenth century. Prisoners of war were sold to slavers, which resulted in more than twelve million African men, women, and children being sent into the Atlantic trade. Both Old Bridget and Nancy, who were captured as children, carried the blueprints for a revolution.[1]

Decades after their arrival in Virginia, Bridget's grandson and Nancy's son Nat Turner would lead the most successful slave revolt in America, and turn a young nation on its head. Two generations removed from West African soil, Turner undoubtedly retained much of his foremothers' ways. Their cultures, steeped in centuries of tradition, transported through trauma and plight, birthed a distinct African-American identity.

Two generations removed from West African soil, Turner undoubtedly retained much of his foremothers' ways.

Virginia's enslaved population was ethnically diverse, spoke several different languages, and practiced a variety of religions. Planters wanted their slaves to assimilate with one another, which they did in slave quarters, where varied cultures—Ibo, Yoruba, Akan, and others—found ways to come together regardless of their disputed pasts. This emerging African-American identity was complex and relied upon oral histories to maintain strong connections to West African culture. Old Bridget and Nancy knew of their ethnic identities, and with that knowledge came a tradition of strength and determination.

In Nate Parker's *The Birth of a Nation*, these cultural connections are both blatant and subtle. Nat Turner was a preacher, and as such the film leans on obvious signifiers of Christianity: the crosses, the Bible, and the churches. However, the iconography of West African spiritual beliefs saturate the film as well. The more familiar the viewer is with diasporic culture, the more vivid these scenes are. The late scholar Dr. VeVe Clark used the term "diasporic literacy" to explain the ability to see superimposed cultural

---

1 Stephen B. Oates, *The Fires of Jubilee: Nat Turner's Fierce Rebellion* (New York: Perennial, 1975), 7–12; and Peter H. Wood, "Nat Turner: The Unknown Slave as Visionary Leader," in *Black Leaders of the Nineteenth Century*, eds. Leon Litwack and August Meier (Urbana: University of Illinois Press, 1988), 21–42.

manifestations in the African diaspora.[2] To view *The Birth of a Nation* without diasporic literacy is to see it through a colonial gaze, riddled with misunderstandings.

Before the opening credits, Turner's mother rushes him into the woods, where they find a healer surrounded by women covered in white ash. The ash covering their half-bare bodies symbolizes the ancestral world. In many traditional West African societies, women were the ones responsible for life (birth) and death (funerals). Covering their bodies in white ash allowed them to make direct contact with the ancestors, and carry out rituals of passing or crossing over. Members of this particular community, marooned in the nearby Great Dismal Swamp, were able to retain much of their African roots. They ran away from their enslavers and created distinct communities, harbored away from the experiences of the plantation South.

Old Bridget, as an elder, surely told tales of her homeland and of her ancestors and likely passed on to Nate beliefs, rooted in the West African traditions, that the ancestors were not dead, but rather their spirits watched over the living, and the line between death and life was fluid. Parker employs this as well in the scenes where the young

They ran away from their enslavers and created distinct communities, harbored away from the experiences of the plantation South.

Nat is standing alongside the adult Nat, and angel-type spirits appear in his visions. Many enslaved Africans and African-Americans practiced a mixture of Christianity and traditional West African religion, though most planters forced their enslaved laborers to convert to Christianity as a mode of assimilation and control. Some aspects of Christianity were easily superimposed onto their cosmologies, allowing for a mask of obedience that allowed them to continue to practice their religion. In Catholic colonies West African orishas were merged with and masked as saints, developing synchronized

---

2 VeVe Clark, "Developing Diaspora Literacy and Marasa Consciousness," in Hortense Spillers, ed., *Comparative American Identities: Race, Sex, and Nationality in the Modern Text* (New York: Routledge, 1991), 40–61.

RIGHT

Script page from *The Birth of a Nation*.

ABOVE

Nate directs the scene depicting what's highlighted in the script.

5 CONTINUED: 6/15/15 - YELLOW 3
5

Nat looks terrified as Nancy removes his shirt. Ezekiel inspects Nat's arms and back before arriving to his chest.

The Elders nudge in, the mouthing of passionate prayer never ceasing. Ezekiel points a thin finger to the boy's sternum.

ANGLE ON THREE SLIGHTLY RAISED KNOTS.

EZEKIEL (CONT'D)
(In the time of our ancestors, the cycle of our people lay in the hands of the children... A man's position was left to the signs of the maker. Children bearing marks were presented before counsel. It was there they were given their assignments in the tribe- assignments that would last a lifetime...)

He points to the first bump on the Nat's chest.

EZEKIEL (CONT'D)
(Wisdom...)
(the second bump)
(Courage...)
(the third)
(Vision...)
(a long beat)
(This boy holds the Holy marks of our ancestors past... He was born to be a prophet.)

At the word **PROPHET**, the surrounding Elders' bodies arch and rock, the intensity of their prayers growing to fever pitch.

We PUSH IN on Nat as he struggles to digest the magnitude of his words. CLOSER. As divine exaltation fills the surrounding blur, we-

CUT TO BLACK

SUPER: BASED ON A TRUE STORY

6 INT. BARN/SLAVE CHURCH - DAY 6

Sunlight cuts through crooked slats, casting golden lines across the dirt floor. Whispers lead toward a corner where we find SEVERAL SHADOWED FIGURES crouched in the darkness.

(CONTINUED)

religions throughout the diaspora. In Virginia, this cultural intersection manifested in the development of hoodoo, a form of West African religion used within a Protestant colony. There were hoodoo practitioners and healers throughout the state. Whites were well aware of them, and oftentimes relied on their powers for their own spiritual and health needs.

The Great Awakening may have increased the percentage of *self-identified* Christian slaves, but even in the nineteenth century, enslaved folks heavily relied on their ancestors for protection and faith. While Nat Turner was indeed a Christian preacher, he was inarguably rooted in a more complex cosmology, one that leaned on more than belief in God; it relied on protection from the ancestors as well. His intense visions throughout the film directly reference this. Additionally, the use of the colors blue and white are noteworthy as they carried incredible significance to enslaved communities, representing the ancestral world and the passing through water to the other side. The courage it took to plan and execute his revolution exemplifies his faith in a complex belief system larger than just Christianity. The ancestors walked with him in life and death; crossing that line in death meant he would have more power to help those living than he did as a man on earth. He must have known he was standing in the shadows of the millions of slaves who came before him, and that they were with him on earth as spiritual protectors.

MATERIALITY and MEMORY

To underestimate the material world of enslaved Africans is to ignore their culture. African captives were typically robbed of their belongings, but some were able to keep remnants of their material world with them through the Middle Passage and onto plantations. Cowry shells, beads, jewelry, and pipes were commonly carried over the Atlantic on the bodies of enslaved Africans. These little things represented their status, history, ethnicity, rites of passage, and cultural identities—but mostly a sense of heritage.

When Turner gives Cherry the gold mask, it represents more than a family heirloom. That gold signifies the kingdoms that ruled West and Central Africa before and during the slave trade, kingdoms that were at war when the Portuguese began trading guns for prisoners. American history, as it is told now, depends on underplaying the historical wealth of African people, positioning them as nameless enslaved bodies during the "era of slavery." History textbooks begin telling the history of black people as slaves, as if their history was always in conversation with whites, a common and highly problematic assumption.

Enslaved folks invested a tremendous amount in the rituals of death, and material culture was central to these moments as well.

Beyond the gold mask, Parker continues to draw on material culture to represent African heritage and cosmologies in the film. In the wedding scene between Cherry and Nat, she is adorned with cowry shells. These shells were brought from West Africa on the bodies of slaves and undoubtedly reminded them of their homeland. These cowry shells were also used as currency, decoration, and as religious items. Shells, colored white and being from the sea, represented the spiritual world of the ancestors. Tradition said that when you died, your spirit passed through water to get to the other side. Shells, as such, were some of the ultimate signifiers of the diaspora, the crossroads, and the ancestors. Cherry wearing them in a crown during a rite of passage, a wedding, speaks directly to the lineage of the community.

Enslaved folks invested a tremendous amount in the rituals of death, and material culture was central to these moments as well. When Nat's grandmother Bridget passes away, she is buried with her belongings and a cross carved to represent her native land of Ghana. This cross, in its intentional aesthetic hybridity, represents the final crossroads for both her and Turner. Bridget's entrance into the spiritual realm allows her to become his protector. The cross as tombstone symbolizes Christianity and a death in the bonds of enslavement, while directly evoking African iconography and cosmology. It is this final tragedy that propels Turner to choose his fate. The ancestors were there with him at the crossroads.

The Birth of a Nation tells a complex story that counters the mainstream slavery

> The Birth of a Nation *presents an unapologetic glimpse into American history, something that will inspire a more sober understanding of our past and the ways in which the legacies of both slavery and white supremacy are still woven into the fabric of our nation.*

narrative. The film has resurrected Nat Turner at a time when America itself is at a crossroads. Nat Turner, one of the most controversial and misunderstood men in American history, is alive in our collective consciousness and is providing a catalyst for change. To understand Turner is to understand his Akan roots; his devotion to his ancestors, his family, and his God; and his path to the crossroads. Turner was not simply a "slave preacher"; he was a complex man with a conviction larger than his torturous world in Southampton County.

PART IV

The Film

The Crew Reflects

Edited by Dominic Patten

HENRY JACKSON

COMPOSER

I read the script, and could see what a passion project this was from the get-go because Nate was extremely honest in how he wanted to tell the story and why he wanted to make the film. He said, "Look all I've got is this script, my vision, and the rest we'll just somehow make happen." I got the impression he thought I might be somewhat disinterested because it wasn't a Hollywood blockbuster in the vein of my

previous work on the Captain America films. I explained to him that the reverse was true—that it would be a privilege to work on the picture. We agreed we would somehow get hold of a budget to produce, arrange, and record the score.

Nate, to his credit, is one of those people who just believes anything and everything is possible. He said, "Henry, you write whatever music you think is appropriate for this film. Imagine it was just any other regular situation, and whether that means a full orchestra or full gospel choir or children's choir or solo players, whatever it is you think it needs, just do it."

It was sort of a leap of faith, and I'm very glad that it did happen because the nature of the film absolutely warrants that trust. By the time you get to the end of the film, it justifies the use of the symphony orchestra and all the rest of it. Nate was true to his word, it all happened and we did indeed record America's finest players at Fox Studios.

The battle sequence at the end is the most powerful part of the film for me in terms of the music because it's so different from a battle climax that you might expect in a giant Hollywood blockbuster. It was very important to get the balance right and not allow the audience's emotions to become carnal or vengeful. In *The Birth of a Nation*, the battle scene is actually a spiritual scene in which Nat Turner, who is by then surrounded by his trusty few, knows that they are involved in a sacrifice and that their uprising is

It was very important to get the balance right and not allow the audience's emotions to become carnal or vengeful.

probably doomed. It was really important to us that at that moment, the music should not accentuate any of the battle elements or the conflict elements, and instead should be more of a spiritual piece that plays on, accentuates, and develops the themes that viewers have been hearing earlier in the film. And I think we actually managed to achieve that so that when they launch into the fight, that whole section there becomes more like a spiritual conclusion than it does an action conclusion. Plus, it's got the use of the voice that was revealed earlier. It all seems to come together.

It is a score that has many musical and distinct instrumentations, and that's partly because of the richness of the film, and the use of the human voice. I never would have imagined at the beginning that we would be able to have so much diversity, because I felt it would be logistically impossible. But we ended up with a score that had a big Nat Turner theme but also had quite a lot of instrumental variation and texture to it, which I really enjoyed. It's a score that has these schematic flashbacks to Turner's African past. There's some African woodwinds and African percussion and there's also solo cello. There's a gospel choir, there's a children's choir, and there's a solo singer. There's the full use of the symphony orchestra.

The orchestra performing the score at the Fox Theater.

The atmosphere surrounding this project was different from any other film on which I've worked. I found in the composition and in the writing that Nate sort of pushed me into a corner, one that, in the end, I loved being in, where there were to be no musical tricks and everything had to be of the highest level of spiritual honesty. Everything was musically exposed and musically honest all the time. That has some musical consequences because of the honesty of the subject matter and the authenticity of it. I don't know what people will think when I say this, but it may be some of the most honest music I've written.

ELLIOT DAVIS

CINEMATOGRAPHER

We wanted the look of the film to be strong—we went with an Arriflex Alexa 2.40 widescreen format, which is essentially Super 35. We were both attracted to that camera's ability to tell this story the way we had imagined, which is with a cool, modern, desaturated look. It is much closer to black and white—very dramatic and representative of our technological world. This desaturated look was further manipulated in post-production in order to reflect the subjective content of the story. When you look at photos from previous wars in history up to Vietnam, the Great Depression, and the Civil Rights movement, they're not in color. They're in black and white.

As in all good design, where form follows function, I always tried to make sure I understood what the intent of a scene was so it had the proper form. If the form didn't match what the subtext of the shot was supposed to be about then we didn't do it, even if it was the most beautiful thing. So I passed up many beautiful images in this film to get the right shot. We got the ones that were important, that expressed what was supposed to be said. In that sense, visually, it's very streamlined.

The A-list crew with which I worked performed beyond anybody's expectations. I was conscious of time while shooting because we didn't have any more than ten or fifteen minutes to do a shot since Nate was so focused and so intent on us getting everything filmed that was in his head. I understood his anxiety because he lived with this project for many years and he wanted to make sure all his ideas were included.

Under Nate's direction, I went with my intuition as a guide. When you have feelings about something, it's usually a good idea to recognize them because they guide you in the right direction. I wanted to get everything that Nate wanted, so I asked myself, how could I do that? First of all, I went with very high-concept lighting as a way of subjectively telling the story and trying to satisfy the speed that was required. This

was an important contributor to the "naturalistic expressionism" that the film exhibits. Sometimes I turned on one big light and saw that it was all that was required. Thinking like that helped deliver the high artistic level and efficiency that Nate wanted. For me it was just a couple big lights with a little bit of fill back or the concept of lighting something in a certain way that lit something completely. Like you turn on a light and boom, it's lit but it's very striking.

Nate was a tremendous motivator for the crew, which helped create a personal connection between the crew and him. Nate motivated the crew to feel like they were part of a bigger picture, with something important to say. He instilled in them a link between the past and the present, which made the film relevant for everyone.

FRANCINE JAMISON-TANCHUCK

COSTUME DESIGNER

I got a call from Nate Parker asking me my availability. He discussed this project that he was bringing to fruition, *The Birth of a Nation*, and he wanted to have the person who costume-designed *Glory* to do his film. We were probably on the phone at least two hours discussing the film and where he was at that particular point. From the very first time that I spoke with him, I knew this project was special and it intrigued me. I was scheduled to go work on something else. But, I thought, I'll do this instead; it just sounded wonderful to me.

When I first spoke with Nate, he said he wanted that realism of *Glory* for his movie. We had just eight weeks in prep before we started rolling film. Even before the movie was green-lit, I went into my research mode. Always a history buff, I already had a small library of research that included what I had collected from the work I did on *Glory*, but I also looked at museum collections, art pieces, and of course, drawings.

There's hardly any artwork or pictures of Nat Turner. I don't know if they were all

destroyed because of what happened in the day or if any ever existed at all. What you do see in the two pictures that depict him is Nat in a pullover, a cream hopsack shirt, or woven shirt, and his pants, which look like they were rough cut.

I thought it would be a good thing to put Nat Turner in a kind of cowhide, rough-looking pant because then you can age it really well. It can look worn and aged, and it gives a very good sense of the textures of the period. I was showing all of that to Nate, even going so far as to rough the leather itself so he could see how it was going to appear. As he really liked it, we decided to go in that direction. We were able to find old boots at the costume house that were already aged down and old hats that we had to just take a little further. Other items—his shirts, for example—had to be designed and made.

My family comes out of the South, out of Alabama, and there's a rural look from the area with which I was familiar. Other nuances I pulled from my research.

When you're looking at the slave masters, one of the main things they had was land that had to be worked, and sometimes they worked it, too. As a result, their clothing had to be made to last or be very functional so they could do whatever they had to do. Plantation families like the ones in the film, who worked their land, handed down their clothes, once they had worn them out, to their slaves. In addition, some of the slaves were really good at making clothing, sewing and weaving, so that was something else to take into consideration when designing the costumes. I had to show the planter class wearing clothes that were comfortable and yet durable, and the slaves wearing hand-me-downs as well as clothes they made themselves.

Beyond the material look, I was affected emotionally as I was designing the costumes; I couldn't help but think of the characters. It's almost as if we went back in time. I started thinking what would these people really do, how would they live? So some things had to be rewoven over and over to reflect the usage, and I wanted to show that in the film.

I do not agree with what Nat Turner did, but I can understand how he got there. For me as an African-American woman, *The Birth of a Nation* is a story about our history, because my family, my great-great-great grandparents, my ancestors, were slaves in this country. It's about bringing history into perspective so that people can really see what has happened in our country and not sweep a lot of it under the table and under the rug. It's about moving forward in certain areas—especially our relationship with each other, whether we are African-American, European American, Native American, whatever the case may be. I think more films probably need to tell our story of our country. So I hope people will look at the film and try to understand that perspective. Some people may say the film is opening up old wounds, but I don't think that is so. People really need to know; otherwise history has a way of repeating itself, especially if people start becoming very insensitive.

Once it's in the foreground, then dialogue starts. That's what all of the crew were talking about when we were making *The Birth of a Nation*. We had such a diverse crew and everyone got along wonderfully. We all knew that this was a story that had to be told.

TURNER PLANTATION
SLAVE QUARTERS

GEOFFREY KIRKLAND

PRODUCTION DESIGNER

I believe that production design should be like a good child. It should be seen and not heard. To me, that describes the importance of not having the production design overtake the story and the characters. The film should never be about your set. It's just a part of that world in which the characters live. Rather, it's very important to know your characters; otherwise you can't design an environment for them.

We had only four weeks from the get-go, which is no time, and we were limited by money, but the process here was like many films: You read the script, you have a story you need to tell, you see who and what the characters are, you see what the background of the story is, and you do your research accordingly. As for the physical set, sometimes you find things that exist already and you make them work for you. In the old days they would line the sets up on the stage and the guys would spend time aging them down. We didn't have enough time to do that on this film. So we had to find locations that felt right. I had to define what we were going to do, and I did a lot of scouting with Nate.

LEFT/RIGHT
Sketches provided by production designer Geoffrey Kirkland.

I also did sketches for Nate when I thought them necessary. He should have probably gotten more than he got, but I could only do so much under the circumstances. We centered our place on this one plantation, and that became our studio in a way. On that, we built the slave cabins and barn, which we had to play as two barns, one of which was a church, where Nat Tuner preached on two different plantations.

The time of Nat Turner's uprising was mysterious because it predates the media in certain respects. There was only the written word and a few paintings and engravings that illustrated the time. It wasn't until after the Civil War that the camera started churning out everything you wanted to know. So it became a question of filling in the dots. For stuff that you can't really ever totally define, you use your common sense and you exercise empathy. It's hard for a white guy from England to empathize with how the slaves actually lived. But knowing what you know, what's a given, you start building your pictures. In this case, I had a really good start because Nate had done so much already.

I could ask Nate a question about anything and he had an answer. All the prep time was just a joy because he knew the subject intimately. It went on that way until the first day of shooting. There he was: dressed, made up, ready to roll. But somehow he still had time to walk around the crew and give everybody a hug, and that happened every day. He had as much time for the camera boys as he did for me. That was the amazing thing, the connectedness. I felt a tremendous connection with him.

W.J. RUFFIN
FEED
GROVE POINT MARKET.
OATS
BARLEY
BRAN
HAY
PRESTONS
FEED AND SEED
W.J. RUFFIN
GENERAL STORE

And out of the throne proceeded lightnings and thunderings and voices: and *there were* ſeven lamps of fire burning before the throne, which are the ſeven Spirits of God.

6 And before the throne *there was* a ſea of glaſs like unto cryſtal: and in the midſt of the throne, and round about the throne, *were* four beaſts full of eyes before and behind.

7 And the firſt beaſt *was* like a lion, and the ſecond beaſt like a calf, and the third beaſt had a face as a man, and the fourth beaſt *was* like a flying eagle.

8 And the four beaſts had each of them ſix wings about *him*; and *they were* full of eyes within: and they reſt not day and night, ſaying, Holy, holy, holy, Lord God Almighty, which was, and is, and is to come.

9 And when thoſe beaſts give glory and honour and thanks to him that ſat on the throne, who liveth for ever and ever,

10 The four and twenty elders fall down before him that ſat on the throne, and worſhip him that liveth for ever and ever, and caſt their crowns before the throne, ſaying,

11 Thou art worthy, O Lord, to receive glory and honour and power: for thou haſt created all things, and for thy pleaſure they are and were created.

CHAP. V.

The book with the ſeven ſeals, &c.

AND I ſaw in the right hand of him that ſat on the throne a book written within and on the backſide, ſealed with ſeven ſeals.

2 And I ſaw a ſtrong angel proclaiming with a loud voice, Who is worthy to open the book, and to looſe the ſeals thereof?

3 And no man in heaven nor in earth, neither under the earth, was able to open the book, neither to look thereon.

4 And I wept much, becauſe no man was found worthy to open and to read the book, neither to look thereon.

5 And one of the elders ſaith unto me, Weep not: behold, the Lion of the tribe of Juda, the Root of David, hath prevailed to open the book, and to looſe the ſeven ſeals thereof.

6 And I beheld, and, lo, in the midſt of the throne and of the four beaſts, and in the midſt of the elders, ſtood a Lamb as it had been ſlain, having ſeven horns and ſeven eyes, which are the ſeven Spirits of God ſent forth into all the earth.

7 And he came and took the book out of the right hand of him that ſat upon the throne.

8 And when he had taken the book, the four beaſts and four and twenty elders fell down before the Lamb, having every one of them harps, and golden vials full of odours, which are the prayers of ſaints.

9 And they ſung a new ſong, ſaying, Thou art worthy to take the book, and to open the ſeals thereof: for thou waſt ſlain, and haſt redeemed us to God by thy blood out of every kindred, and tongue, and people, and nation;

10 And haſt made us unto our God kings and prieſts: and we ſhall reign on the earth.

11 And I beheld, and I heard the voice of many angels round about the throne and the beaſts and the elders: and the number of them was ten thouſand times ten thouſand, and thouſands of thouſands;

12 Saying with a loud voice, Worthy is the Lamb that was ſlain to receive power, and riches, and wiſdom, and ſtrength, and honour, and glory, and bleſſing.

13 And every creature which is in heaven, and on the earth, and under the earth, and ſuch as are in the ſea, and all that are in them, heard I ſaying, Bleſſing, and honour, and glory, and power, *be* unto him that ſitteth upon the throne, and unto the Lamb for ever and ever.

14 And the four beaſts ſaid, Amen. And the four *and* twenty elders fell down and worſhipped him that liveth for ever and ever.

CHAP. VI.

The opening of the ſeals, &c.

AND I ſaw when the Lamb opened one of the ſeals, and I heard, as it were the noiſe of thunder, one of the four beaſts ſaying, Come and ſee.

2 And I ſaw, and behold a white horſe: and he that ſat on him had a bow; and a crown was given unto him: and he went forth conquering, and to conquer.

3 And when he had opened the ſecond ſeal, I heard the ſecond beaſt ſay, Come and ſee.

4 And there went out another horſe *that was* red: and *power* was given to him that ſat thereon to take peace from the earth, and that they ſhould kill one another: and there was given unto him a great ſword.

5 And when he had opened the third ſeal, I heard the third beaſt ſay, Come and ſee. And I beheld, and lo a black horſe; and he that ſat on him had a pair of balances in his hand.

6 And I heard a voice in the midſt of the four beaſts ſay, A meaſure of wheat for a penny, and three meaſures of barley for a penny; and *ſee* thou hurt not the oil and the wine.

7 And

OPPOSITE AND TOP RIGHT
Nat Turner's actual Bible, which is housed in the African American Museum of the Smithsonian.

CENTER RIGHT AND BELOW
The sword Nat Turner used in the rebellion, now housed in the Southampton County Historical Society, Courtland, Virginia.

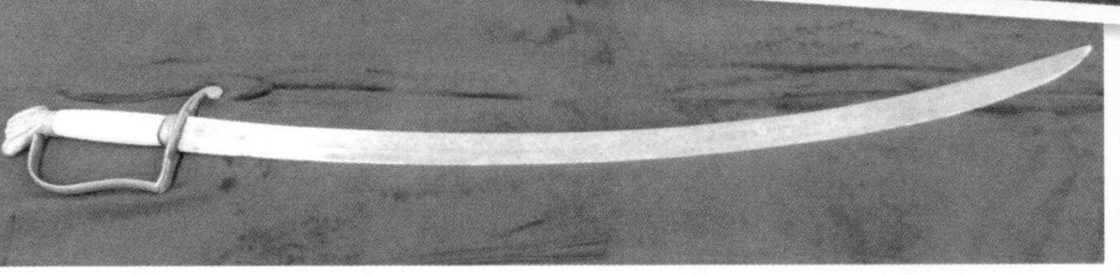

Commentary by the Cast

Edited by Briana Rodriguez

THE LOVE STORY: *An Interview with* AJA NAOMI KING

CHERRY

We first see Aja Naomi King in *The Birth of a Nation* hollow-eyed and hunched over on an auction block. You'd be forgiven if it took you several minutes to place her as the same actor who portrays Michaela Pratt, the over-achieving law student on ABC's *How to Get Away with Murder*. For this film, King, a classically trained California native, confronted a new side to her craft as Cherry, Nat Turner's wife.

How you first came in to read for this film is really interesting. You sat down with Nate before and had a Skype session about how to approach Cherry. What was it like to have that kind of introduction to this character and to the person who would ultimately cast you?

AJA NAOMI KING: **As an actor you don't get that. Ever. Usually you're walking into the room blind. I thought there was something really special about that, that he would take the time so I would have a better idea and more tools. He told me what he would** like me to read—a slave narrative—and that really felt empowering, as in, *Oh, so you want me to be really good at this when I go into the room? You want me to have a lived-in experience already, versus having to discover that later on the spot during the audition.*

What did you take to heart most deeply in that initial conversation?

I remember him talking about her strength—that was a big one for me. Not that she was infallible, not that she didn't have any kind of vulnerability, because he really spoke about her humanity: We are well-rounded human beings. We're not just beasts of burden. We are people, but she's a fighter.

An actor's face is one of their biggest tools, yet in one first scene, Cherry, after having survived this barbaric beating at the hands of Cobb, is unrecognizable. You were limited in how you could use your face, yet it's one of the most powerful scenes in the film. How did you feel knowing such a pivotal moment would be coming from beneath so much makeup?

Any kind of production I've done where the character gets beat up, someone paints a black eye on your face or applies some dried blood on you, and you still have use of your face to tell different parts of the story. But in this, I was under this prosthetic. I had no idea we were going to do all that! I *felt* as if I'd been beaten upon. I could barely see Nate, but I could feel him. I could feel his energy and I could catch his eye.

I couldn't gauge what any sort of movement would look like or how it would read on camera. So what I did draw from? From the breath and how we speak. When I do move to touch Nat Turner's face, just knowing how hard it would be to lift my arm, but how necessary it would have been to let him know it's still me, that I had not been destroyed. There's an effort in all of that, and that's what I was engaging with in that moment. That's when I realized where the story was.

It's such a real moment between them. Another moment is when Nat Turner approaches Cherry about organizing the rebellion. It almost seems as if he acknowledges that his mission and dedication to his people are bigger than the love the two of them have.

I actually think it's fueled by the love that Cherry and Nat had built. Something about understanding love, feeling love, having love, fuels you to sacrifice for a greater kind of love: the love of your people, the love of all mankind.

You've said before that you really idolize your costar Viola Davis for her fearlessness after she exposed herself and her bare face, for example, on How to Get Away with Murder. *Cherry comes so far over the course of the film, but there's such a rawness when the audience first sees her on that auction block. How vulnerable did you feel in that moment?*

Filming on an actual plantation, just knowing your history, it's easy to get into that space. It becomes something you can allow in a little bit, but something you kind of have to fight against because you might be swallowed by it. I was genuinely a little afraid because I didn't know how I was going to feel walking onto that land. I soon found out. In that first scene, stepping up onto an auction block—it was like blood memory. The spirits of all those who had stepped onto that auction block before enter you. And I was holding on to my backstory, but I was also being flooded with the truth of that moment. It was about remembering Cherry's strength and remembering everything she had been through, so I didn't fall apart, because she is strong. But that was heavy. It's something you can't deny, you can't avoid, so you have to allow it, you have to accept it, and live in it.

You trained at Yale School of Drama for your master's in fine arts. Is there a piece of that training that you found most useful in finding Cherry?

We were taught to approach our characters in a kind of scientific way. Before we even begin trying to live inside of a character, we have to break down their entire history—their physical, emotional, spiritual, and actual history. Who am I? Who am I to myself? Who am I to others? Who am I emotionally? And then once all *that* work is done, once that very clinical breakdown is completed, then you can start to do the other work, the living inside of it.

For Cherry I had to create a little diary, a little story of her life, something that she would never share with anyone, but that explained exactly how she got to the first moment you saw her. That's what I needed. You can't find a lot about her in books or elsewhere, which is a little freeing in a sense, because then I got to create a persona and circumstances to which I could emotionally attach. Then it was mine and only mine.

You didn't see the original The Birth of a Nation *until you were in college at UC Santa Barbara. How do you think seeing a film like this 2016 version when you were young would've affected you?*

I grew up being maybe either the only black person or one of two black people in my classroom. So when Black History Month rolled around, we were taught we were enslaved and we marched for civil rights and we waited for others to grant us permission to live as human beings. The end. So to see a movie like this, where you get to watch a black man be a warrior for good, be a hero for his people—that would've been so self-affirming. It would've been so impactful for me to have a different version of our history. There's something about the idea that we were waiting for permission that has always bothered me. What is so beautiful about this film is that it opens up the notion in your mind that we had our warriors. We had our fighters. We had our rebels and rebellions.

It's important to understand how powerful film can be; we learned that when the 1915 *The Birth of a Nation* reignited the Ku Klux Klan. It was a film that caused people to walk out of movie theaters and look for black people to terrorize. Yes, a film can do all that, and I'm excited to see the kind of reaction people will have from watching this film. What will be the change? When people walk out of theaters after watching this, what will they want to do for themselves and for others in their lives?

"Love is the kind of thing that will drive you into the battlefield, and there's something so precious about that, to understand something so intimately, you know how important it is to preserve the very nature of it. . . . I think [Nat's] is that kind of love that will make you sacrifice your own precious, intimate love."

THROUGH THE LOOKING GLASS:

An Interview with ARMIE HAMMER

SAMUEL TURNER

As Nat's childhood friend and slave master Samuel Turner, Armie Hammer plays the nuances of a man trapped in his circumstances. Known for his duality (he played both the Winklevoss twins in 2010's *The Social Network*), Hammer underscores Samuel's building desperation to prove himself a worthy heir to the Turner name. Here he talks about the eye-opening experience of walking through downtown Savannah, Georgia, and how his own family history helped him see Samuel more clearly.

Your great-grandfather was oil tycoon Armand Hammer. Coming from a well-known family yourself, how did you initially relate to Samuel's desire to represent his bloodline and "make the Turner name mean something again"?

ARMIE HAMMER: That part required one hundred percent acting. It wasn't anything I was interested in; if it were, I wouldn't have dropped out of high school, I would've gone to college like my parents wanted me to, and I probably would've been working for the family, but that wasn't for me. As someone who got away from that I understood how Samuel could become trapped by it, which is essentially what happened. His hand has been played for him. He has to do this. He has to make his Turner name mean something or else the family house would continue to fall apart. He'd have to sell off everything. He would be an embarrassment in the community, and for Samuel that was a big deal. Fortunately for me it wasn't, but I see how it could be for a character like that.

In terms of your craft, did you learn anything new while playing Samuel?

Definitely, because you learn something on every project, hopefully. I would say more than anything, I learned to kind of push myself in a direction that I hadn't really gone before.

What direction is that?

There's hopefully a very sort of subtle but dramatic shift that goes on with him. Initially, he and Nat are brothers. They grew up together, they literally played together as kids. After Samuel's dad dies, it's "Nat is yours. He's your property now. You own Nat now." "What? Nat? You mean the kid I played with growing up? My friend?" "Yup, he's yours. Now you also have to keep everything running. Now you have to keep the crops growing." He was sort of forced into this thing, and he ends up very different from how he first starts.

Take us through of the conversations you had with Nate before your first day on set.

I had my research phase where I was talking to him throughout. I would call him with things that I learned, interesting tidbits I'd picked up: "Nate, did you know that white kids and black kids who were slaves at the time grew up together until about the age of eleven or twelve, and then they would pull them apart?". . . I actually hired a professional researcher, whom I've worked with on every project, and she went and dug up everything. I had the Turner family diaries. I had the ledgers where they kept how much grain they harvested each year, how they ran the house, who was appointed to which place. I even had numbers for how much they actually paid [for Nat]. They kept efficient records at the time so you can find a ton of stuff—you just have to sift through all that.

The character of Samuel was an amalgamation of two actual people: There was a Samuel Turner, but there was also another guy that married one of the Turner daughters, and the character Samuel is an amalgamation of the two men.

How did you determine what to take from each person?

I had the historical research of these two guys, but at the same time I had the script, which was so good. Each character was so fleshed out and so full of humanity that even this slave owner, who you would look at and think, *I would never do that*, is fleshed out such that you see the progression of this character. It was less about me being the character of Samuel saying my lines, and it was more about Nate having fleshed it out on paper. It's just my job now to make this come alive.

This isn't about slavery, this is about the country that we live in now, which was very much so shaped by this time.

You've called this a life-changing experience. What made it that way for you?

I got to Savannah, Georgia, and Nate says, "I want you to come take a walk with me." He says, "Just pay attention to whoever looks at you." We walked around downtown for about an hour, and when we got back to the studio and he asked, "How many people looked you in the eye?" and I said, "Quite a few," he asked, "How many white people looked you in the eye as you walked past them?" And I said, "Most, if not all [of] them?" Then he asked, "How many black people looked you in the eye?" Very few did. He said, "Okay, zero white people when we were walking around looked at me and none of the black people looked at me, either."

It was a jarring introduction to this world that I had no idea still existed. We say we're past it and we say it doesn't exist anymore and we ask, well, what's the problem? That experience in itself epitomizes what the issue is right now. This isn't about slavery, this is about the country that we live in now, which was very much so shaped by this time.

BLOOD TIES:
An Interview with AUNJANUE ELLIS

NANCY TURNER

For *The Birth of a Nation* Aunjanue Ellis inhabited the complex role of Nat Turner's mother. The actor is best known for her film roles in *Ray*, *The Help*, and *Men of Honor*. Most recently she's appeared on ABC's *Quantico* as the assistant director of the FBI Academy, Miranda Shaw, and the Canadian six-part television miniseries *The Book of Negroes*.

You've played so many strong female characters in a time when many other women are seeking and demanding more roles in the same vein. Nancy Turner is a courageous woman in her own right, so I'm curious as to which of your past roles spoke most to her?

AUNJANUE ELLIS: **Every time I do something I try to start from zero and examine what the character and I have in common and what we don't. Whatever points of trauma or happiness that I can pull from my life, I try to use that. Since what Nate wrote was so strong and so complemented my feelings that this kind of story is important and needs to be told, particularly at this moment in our history, I pulled less from my acting history and more from my personal history, my personal reservoir.**

And what were those similarities and differences between you and Nancy when it came to that personal history?

Nate and I had a lot of discussions before we started shooting. He talked a lot about enslaved people, the things they did just in terms of the mannerisms they employed to survive; one, for example, was the habit of looking down and doing things that didn't draw attention to their real emotions, how they really felt. And we also talked about how

There's reclamation of our history
that we have to do, and that reclamation
has to be on everybody's part.

they would do that and be subversive at the same time. Thinking along those terms was very challenging for me, specifically in one scene where Nancy Turner's plantation owner [played by Penelope Ann Miller] tells her that she is going to take Nat to the house to live. This is a woman saying, "I'm going to take your son from you." So having a modern sensibility, knowing how I would feel about that, but then having to repress all that real emotion that you would actually feel, that's the difference.

You are an activist in your own right. You made a big statement about the Confederate bars and stars on the Mississippi flag on the red carpet at the NAACP Awards, with a dress that read, "Take it down, Mississippi." How do you see and hope The Birth of a Nation *furthers the conversations you've already started?*

I don't think anybody has a choice, but I *really* don't have the luxury of choice in this because I live in Mississippi, where a Confederate flag, the flag of the KKK, will probably be hanging from some place I'm going to today. That has worn on me and worn on me since I was a child. The last couple of years I've been very lucky to be involved in projects like [*The Birth of a Nation*], where I play characters or a family member of a character who felt like they did not have a choice—there is no choice in this. The fact that we have the flag of a terrorist organization, the flag of the Confederacy, another nation, and we fly it on public property, on federal property, that's not a Mississippi problem—that says something about this country.

I feel like there's reclamation of our history that we have to do, and that reclamation has to be on everybody's part. People, throughout the course of American history, have had to constantly hold America accountable for its promises, and Nat Turner, that's what he did. What I'm excited about and what I'm hoping for is a gradual turn. Not one thing is going to make it happen, not two things are going to make it happen. But I'm hoping that, for a moment, we can start examining ourselves through each other's eyes.

A STARK CONTRAST:
An Interview with
COLMAN DOMINGO

HARK

Colman Domingo, known most recently for his starring role as Victor Strand on *Fear the Walking Dead*, plays Hark, Nat Turner's right hand during the historic 1831 rebellion. The award-winning performer speaks on the surreal experience of watching himself on screen as Hark and the danger he felt while shooting *The Birth of a Nation*.

You've made a career portraying characters who tackle racially charged injustices. You played civil rights activist Ralph Abernathy in the Martin Luther King, Jr., story Selma. *You were nominated for a Tony for your performance as Mr. Bones in* The Scottsboro Boys, *a true retelling of the story of nine black teenagers falsely accused of rape in 1931. You were in* Lincoln, *too. And now of course you have Hark. What does he mean to your larger canon of work?*

COLMAN DOMINGO: It seems to fall right in place. Even as an artist, when I started this journey, what, twenty-seven years ago? You hope your gifts will be used to make some change in the world, and it started to dawn on me by the time I did *Selma* and from being a part of *Lincoln* and *Lee Daniels' The Butler*, and even to a degree *Fear the Walking Dead*—that these movies are all about our humanity. When I was a younger actor, I used to always question and wonder why I didn't get cast on some crazy show on the WB where I could just make a lot of money. It makes sense to me now that the roles I do receive are in things in which I'm passionately invested.

You've said you're proud to be a creator who takes risks and "walks off the cliff artistically." Was there a point during The Birth of a Nation *where you felt you were doing that?*

We had a lot of night shoots. Night shoots on a plantation, where you just knew there was blood in the soil, which imparted a sense of darkness even in your spirit. You were calling on all this trauma in the air, in the land, in the things that we touched. In response we created a sense of very "well-protected danger." You had to look at someone with whom you were having a meal, whom you loved deeply and who you felt was your brother in arms, this Caucasian brother, but you had to honor who the people they portrayed were in our history, and while filming call each other the worst racial epithets; you have to go and take an axe and drive it into their skull. There had to be a permission granted between us because you knew there was an agreement that you had to do this, because this is the absolute truth of the fabric of America. For me it was in those night shoots where you felt like you were going off a cliff.

You come from a theater background and have showcased an incredible range in that space, for example with your solo show, A Boy and His Soul, *where you play all the characters in your family and then some. What does film bring out of your acting that's different, and specifically in* The Birth of a Nation*? Did you see something new in yourself?*

When I watched it at Sundance, I didn't recognize myself. Today, we have these things that we have built up that tell the world who we are. But the man I played could never have done that. He was marginalized and beaten and downtrodden, and I had to be honest with that interpretation. For me that honesty was about not only playing Hark and his experience, it was playing great-great-grandfathers and uncles and aunts, it was about bringing their spirit into it. So then when I watched it, I understood. I would look at my face and feel like I look older than I am—not that I'm a spring chicken. But usually I see someone who's pretty mellow and happy-go-lucky; that was never an option for Hark, that was always being beaten out of him. This has been a development, something that will carry me into my next stage of career.

I'm seeking the truth more and less artifice. Right after filming, I had to go direct a production of August Wilson's *Seven Guitars*. With every actor, I tried to boil it down, boil it down, to let it be even closer to their experience, to their souls; I took that from this film. I'm trying to let the work be closer not only to myself but to the people whose shoulders I stand on.

I know that you have little formal acting training and you studied journalism. I'm sure that helps with all the research you do for these period pieces. How did your journalism skills play into your process of discovering Hark?

I am a research fiend. I like to research everything I can, and not only about the character—that's thinking small. I like to research what was going on at the time, everything. Even when we got to the set, my questions were: Whose plantation was this at that time? And who was here? I'm an actor who thrives in the moment, but I like to go through the history books. I read biographies, anything I could get, whether it's a book about slave narratives, et cetera. Personally it was important to me that I didn't just play Hark. In portraying him, I wanted to represent all of the Harks, so it was a bit more universal in that way. I was tapping into things about all those men who had to endure these complicated, horrific scenarios in their lives. So, yes, I research a lot.

You grew up in Philadelphia's public school system. I'm curious about the history books you studied when it came to African-American history.

From what I can recall, what I learned was that we were enslaved, and then there was Martin Luther King, and now we're here. When I went to Temple University, I took one African-American Studies class and it changed my life. There was so much that I didn't know. I had questions about why it's African-American history—why isn't it American history? Why is it segregated? It disenfranchises from the start if you segregate it. With *The Birth of a Nation*, we have such a vivid portrayal. I love the idea that films are there to help you interrogate. They're in no way trying to say, "This is absolutely factual." It's art, but it's a useful tool for there to be more examinations of our collective history.

"Even with all the blood, [The Birth of a Nation] *is about love. Nate has written, in essence, a love story. That's the only reason I'm still here, why he's still here: There had to be love, there had to be hope."*

DISAPPEARING ACT:
An Interview with
GABRIELLE UNION

UNNAMED SLAVE WOMAN

Star of BET's *Being Mary Jane* Gabrielle Union took on a small role for *The Birth of a Nation*, as an unnamed slave living on the Turner plantation. Her rape by a visiting slave master is one of the pivotal incidents leading up to Nat's ultimate decision to revolt against their oppressors. Union has no recollection of shooting that scene and explains in this interview why she thinks that is.

A lot of people have said you're unrecognizable and that you really bury yourself in this role.

GABRIELLE UNION: I'm unrecognizable in that there was nothing typical or strategic or planned, which I for sure do elsewhere. I'm a hack most of the time in my work. I know where the eyebrow raise is going. I know where the sexy smirk is going. I know where every single camera is at any given time. My performance is so self-aware, to a point where I'm sure it's detrimental, but with this I had no idea where the camera was because that's not what my journey was about. I just allowed myself to be—and for the record, I think it's weird when actors talk like this.

You've said elsewhere you have no recollection of filming the rape scene. Now that some time has passed since you saw your performance for the first time at Sundance, have you come to any new realizations about your experience in that moment?

It was an amazing, otherworldly experience, and it's stayed that way. I don't know if I'll get those moments back and I'm not exactly sure I need them back. I don't know if I'm capable of handling that. After I walked out of the house in which my character is violated, I only remember applause and tears and everyone hugging me. The weight

of the reality and the honesty of that moment are too much to bear. And I'm okay if I never know. . . . I do remember sitting there next to Colman [Domingo, who plays Hark]—who's much more spiritually connected than I—just joking and praying with our people, which is weird to say, but when I talk to God it's not all fire and brimstone, it's with humor. That's my personality. So I said, "Please don't let the chick from *Bring It On* screw this up!"

Was that actually a part of the prayer you said with Colman or are you just saying that for comedic effect?

No, no! That was part of the prayer to the ancestors! It's interesting because in those moments where I'm talking to our people and our collective people—and I'd like to include Jesus in that—but people who are no longer here, I use humor.

Despite its small size, you've called this the most challenging role you've ever taken. You were shuttling back and forth between Atlanta for Being Mary Jane *and Savannah for* The Birth of a Nation, *but what else made it so trying for you?*

As an aware person, and knowing where we're at now as a nation, in terms of brown people moving through the world freely, I was very cognizant going into the experience of the parallels between where we were nearly two hundred years ago and where we are now. And I was cognizant of the lack of progress and of the presence of our ancestors on the land at that plantation. So it literally felt like one of those times where not a single f—d up detail of our collective history as black people was lost on me. Everything felt very loaded. So by the time I got dropped off on the land, it felt as if I were never alone. Like when they give you buddies at camp, I felt like I had a buddy in terms of our ancestors.

As a survivor of sexual assault, you've said that you wanted to address, with your character, the voicelessness and powerlessness women, but especially African-American women, and especially victims of sexual assault, have historically felt. Expand upon that. And was your and Nate's decision to remove your character's lines a tough call to make?

I've been offered other characters who share the same experience of either being raped on screen or raped as a backstory, and I wasn't interested. What is the larger goal here? It just felt like brutality porn but without a purpose. I tell my story in real life, so what else am I trying to accomplish with it on screen? If I can't accomplish with it more on stage than what I'm already talking about off stage, then why do it? With this I felt like I was able to convey something I haven't done or haven't been able to do in the countless times I talked about my own experience. What I did in that moment from what I've seen is equivalent to twenty years of therapy.

As for having no lines, I can only speak as an actor who has my own show and had other movies coming out. Luckily, like Kevin Hart says—"The way my bank account is set up!"—the way my life is set up, I have so many other ways I feel fulfilled that I don't need to count lines at this stage of my career. My self-esteem allowed me to really do what was best for the character and not for me, and that's both liberating and rare in our town. What's best for the character is also what's best for you and your brand, usually. And as someone who has been raped, you need so many more words than even what was on the page to really convey what that is. There are no words.

Your marriage scene is one of several in the film that vividly call back to African tradition. What did you know about those rituals beforehand?

I didn't have a lot of knowledge in that area. As many times as I'd been back to Africa, I'd never seen anything like that. I got the gist, but in no way, shape, or form was I physically prepared for what we did. And in that moment I just allowed myself to be lifted up by the energy that was in the space and the energy that was present. When I've seen the footage, even what didn't end up in the film, there's a joy in my face that didn't actually exist in my own wedding! And I was happy as hell! I don't know what that is except something that is beyond me.

THE VALUE OF HINDSIGHT:
An Interview with
JACKIE EARLE HALEY

RAYMOND COBB

Oscar nominated actor-director Jackie Earle Haley terrifies as the slave hunter Raymond Cobb. In the past he's tackled other grim and nefarious characters in films such as *Little Children*, *Watchmen*, and *A Nightmare on Elm Street*. He made his directorial debut in 2015 with *Criminal Activities*. A passionate denouncer of racial injustice, the actor talks about his hopes for the film's audience.

What were you surprised to learn when you first came on to The Birth of a Nation?

JACKIE EARLE HALEY: When I first talked to Nate about *The Birth of a Nation* and the role of Cobb, I was surprised—shouldn't have been but I was—to learn that the very first police in this country, their sole job was to police slaves, was to police blacks who weren't where they were supposed to be—they had no other authority. They didn't mess with any white people; everyone was free to do whatever they wanted. I thought that was incredibly telling.

I was drawn to Nate and the screenplay that he wrote. I thought it was an important story to tell. I'd always wondered why there wasn't a rebellion back in the 1800s, and I was surprised to learn that there was. And I certainly wish it had turned out better for the people that rebelled, but it was fascinating to learn that story.

You had your first directorial feature just last year, Criminal Activities, *and acted in the film as a supporter to John Travolta. How did that influence how you came to a set being led by not only another actor, but a fellow actor?*

When I did *The Birth of a Nation*, I had already directed my film, so there was a piece of me that was really identifying with Nate just in the sense that he's directing his first movie and he's starring in it; in mine I didn't star, but I had a good supporting role, so I was really in there rooting for him.

Actors are always a little bit concerned about working with a first-time director, but when we spoke I could tell that this guy knows what he's doing. He'll be able to direct this film. He's not going to be like a deer in the headlights. And sure enough we get to the set and the guy totally knew what he was doing. I was really rooting for him because I'd just experienced this thing myself. I like to say it's *The Birth of a Nation*—but it's also birth of a director, birth of a great writer, and birth of a movie star.

You're well versed in playing dark and villainous characters. Was there ever a time during filming where you as a person felt a real discomfort in your role as this slave hunter?

There's a scene where I go into the family's house and start questioning them and using the n-word. When I first go in, it's uncomfortable, but at the same time, I'm a professional, so I have to commit. You can't be so uncomfortable in a situation that you can't allow yourself to go through it, because you agreed to do this, and you have to own it, and you have to mean it when you're saying it even though you're acting. I was so uncomfortable, but after I did my bit my fellow actors said, "Wow, that's great. We didn't even have to act because we were all scared shitless!" What I found was absolute graciousness in that room. It was the discomfort of going in and playing that character with my fellow actors who were black, shouting the n-word, and more, and they were very supportive. And then that really freed me up even more to play this evil guy. But yes, at first it's kind of tough.

Hopefully this type of story allows us to see clearly into the past and opens our eyes up to what's going on today.

After this film did you find yourself trying to change the things you see in your own life that you identify as injustices?

The best way I can help is to try and help Nate tell this story and to try to find other things and stories that are relevant and be part of that. It's hard to know what to do because the system is so stacked against, especially, our poor neighborhoods, our poor communities, our poor black communities.

I happen to be very passionate about this subject matter. I find myself constantly reading articles and watching the news in disgust at the state of racism today. I read the screenplay and I wanted to help Nate tell this story. I think we can all clearly see, when you take a look at a film like this, which takes place in 1830, now that it's 2016, we can really see the absolute injustice of what was going on back then. Hopefully this type of story allows us to see clearly into the past and opens our eyes up to what's going on today.

A GLASS HALF-FULL:
An Interview with
MARK BOONE JUNIOR

THE REVEREND

Mark Boone Junior has more than 150 acting credits (including seven seasons of *Sons of Anarchy*) to his name. In *The Birth of a Nation* he plays the role of the local reverend who convinces Samuel Turner to rent Nat out to plantation owners hoping to quell the unrest on their lands. Ironically, it's the slave preacher's travels around the county that empower him. Boone discusses shooting one terrifyingly convincing scene and the item that best helped him get into character.

In interviews you've said filming certain scenes during The Birth of a Nation *was transformative, and you came to some frightening realizations while on set. Can you speak on what some of those realizations were?*

MARK BOONE JUNIOR: **I've never had a part in a pre–Civil War film. I've played a lot of Southern people. I was in *Rosewood* [the 1997 film about a racist attack on an African-American community], and that was a rough movie. [John] Singleton put us in a room for a week, ten days, where we just acquainted ourselves with being assholes. . . . That was a very contentious movie, and I played a very, very nasty—to both whites and blacks—historical character.**

In what I recall was actually the first scene that I did, I was walking across the yard with Armie Hammer, who plays Samuel Turner. Jeryl Prescott, who plays Janice, a slave on the Turner plantation, was walking alongside me, and I hadn't even realized I had a glass of water, which I finished, and she filled it up before I knew she was doing that. Her manner was so convincing, and she so manifested that sense of subservience, I didn't have to do anything. There was no acting involved. That power swept over me, as did the

sense of what that would've been like to have that kind of power over people, and to not question it. You didn't question it! And talk about an acting job. It makes you wonder, how could this have ever occurred? That was an amazing experience as a person and an actor. But it totally freaked me out how that power involuntarily swept over me.

There's a scene in the film where there's a battle of biblical citations that justify both the Reverend and Nat's positions. It clarifies even further that Nat is driven purely by the word of God. What was shooting that scene like?

Something has clarified itself so thoroughly for Nat at that moment. It's actually the turning point in the whole movie, and the wake of the indignation comes thundering down upon this man. You see Nat's personal struggle. And you also see that this is where Samuel turns the corner as well.

It was just fantastic to do that scene. It's the one that shows that Nat's ready to march ahead. And for me it's strangely representative of the whole institution of slavery. The church upheld the institution just as individuals, God-fearing Christian people, lived this life of owning people. It's really hard to imagine how this could be. But there it is.

You've done several movies with first-time directors and said you like doing them because (1) you enjoy helping and (2) it's where you feel you really get to act. Knowing you'd have more opportunity to play and dig in than you would on another film, how did you approach your character?

I had some conversations with a dialogue coach and that started this whole sound thing of hearing the character. The wardrobe really helped, too; all of that for me, that's how it all happens. It's like wearing a suit. And that hat! I put that hat on and it was like, Okay, there he is! Plus, just the whole atmosphere of that set. Everything. The idyllic setting, everyone's behavior. It really felt effortless in some way. It all felt like it was supposed to be.

EXPLORING THE GRAY AREA: *An Interview with* PENELOPE ANN MILLER

ELIZABETH TURNER

As the Turner family matriarch, Elizabeth, Penelope Ann Miller is the first to arm Nat with the word of God by putting a Bible in his hand and teaching him to read it. In this interview the Tony- and Golden Globe–nominated actor challenges the notion of pure villainy and pure good in a system that breeds neither.

Nat Turner's a complicated hero figure. How did you sort through the complexities of Nat's ultimate actions both for your character and yourself?

PENELOPE ANN MILLER: **I talked a lot to Nate about that, because it was hard to fully comprehend how this woman could deal with that kind of guilt. Here she has a son who was murdered by the hands of this other man, who she also, I think in a weird way, considered to be a surrogate son. She understood the reasons Nat killed Samuel, and yet he still is her son. It was so complex and really intense. How do you wrestle with those feelings of a mother who has raised a child and then seen another child grow up, a child for whom she is somewhat responsible, and end her own child's life? It's a huge cross to bear. As I prepared, I contemplated how she would have worked through the extent to which she was responsible, too: Did I do something wrong? Was it something I could have prevented if I had protected him differently? And then, where did I go wrong with my own son? It was sometimes hard to wrap my head around what that reality would really be like.**

You studied at HB Studio in New York City. You have a Tony nomination for Our Town. *And you've starred opposite some of our generation's biggest actors—De Niro, Pacino, Brando. What piece of your training or past roles did you find most useful for this film?*

I was doing Neil Simon's *Biloxi Blues* on Broadway, which was directed by Gene Saks, who had done the Neil Simon trilogy of *Brighton Beach*, *Biloxi*, and *Broadway Bound*. Right before I went on for the first performance, he said to me, "Trust your instincts. They're always right." That hit me in a way that I'll never forget. There was something about that, that just made me relax because I thought, *I don't have to try—I can just be, and I can just let whatever takes over, take over.*

And I remember Herbert Berghof, whom I studied with at HB Studio, told me that people gravitate toward children and animals because they're not judging themselves, and they're not trying to be anything but who and what they are. They're just truly in the present moment. That's what I sort of try to do when I work. Berghof said it's the greatest game of make-believe there is.

Did you ever feel like you were taking a risk, whether personally or professionally, portraying a woman on the wrong side of history?

I didn't see it as a risk. I mean, there are certainly a lot of actors who have played people on the wrong side of history. It's our job as actors to portray people both good and bad in order to tell an accurate and compelling story.

Back then, in the 1700s, there were people who were born into slavery, and there were people who were born into being slave owners. They didn't know anything different. They didn't know a different way of life. Elizabeth was a complex character to play, and it's hard to imagine in this day and age what that would be like, but I do feel she had compassion and cared for Nat, perhaps in the only way she knew how. She did teach this young slave to read, which was against the law.

Was there something that surprised you about someone's reaction to or interpretation of the film or Elizabeth?

Nate talked to me a lot about Elizabeth and her compassion and her complexities, but he also warned me that there will be people who will never see my character, Elizabeth, as good, no matter what she does. She still was a slave owner, and that really resonated with me. I realized that it will never be enough, and that is the burden she has to carry

"My greatest hope [for the film is that] it's a reminder for all of us to have that compassion for where we've been, what we've been through, and where we could or couldn't go. We all have choices to make in our lives."

with her for the rest of her life, and that we also have to carry in our history. Maybe by confronting those feelings we can also have compassion. When we talk about healing, hopefully that is where it begins.

Elizabeth tries in her own way to give Nat some privileges. There's a scene where she allows Nat to go and baptize a white man, knowing her son Samuel will greatly disapprove, but she's trying to let Nat do something that's meaningful to him. He later gets whipped for it. Everything she tries to give him doesn't come without severe consequences. There's responsibility in that, and in the choices she makes. However, when you educate someone, you're giving them power—for better or for worse. Look what Nat Turner did, what happened to him, and where we are now: this is his legacy.

THE PATH TO RIGHTEOUSNESS:
An Interview with
ROGER GUENVEUR SMITH

ISAIAH

Roger Guenveur Smith, an Obie- and Peabody Award–winning director, playwright, and actor, brings his talents to the conflicted Isaiah, a house slave with allegiances to both his master and his fellow slaves. In this interview Smith draws parallels between the timing of *Malcolm X*, the Spike Lee film in which he also had a role, and *The Birth of a Nation*, as well as talks about muddying up his boots—literally and figuratively—for the role.

When Isaiah tries to talk Nat out of rebelling, he represents, in many ways, at that moment, the power the system of slavery had over the enslaved and the fear it inspired. And when Jasper tips off the plantation owners, his actions represent the same thing.

ROGER GUENVEUR SMITH: **Yes, but look at the fate of Jasper. Look at how he's transformed in one of the most startling pieces of cinema that I've seen in recent years. This boy, who may have tipped the white slave owners off at that farm, then witnesses the hanging of Nat Turner, is finally transformed into a Union soldier. That's the journey of African people in the Americas. We are exposed to our own degradation. We are tempted to blow the whistle as supporters of the institution that nominally feeds us, and yet we have these grand opportunities for salvation and redemption and liberation. The path to righteousness is not a straight one.**

Isaiah obviously has a job to do and a certain sense of loyalty to his position. But I think Isaiah also has a loyalty to the larger community that he serves. . . . When Nat

kills his master, it's not the loss of the master that he mourns so much as the loss of the community, who will pay the price with hangings and beheadings. Nat Turner pays for his liberating gesture, which is not undertaken without his own ambivalence. He doesn't want to necessarily kill these people. In fact, when he kills his master, he throws up. But this is something he feels is absolutely necessary because he's inspired not only by Scripture but also by life on that plantation.

Did this film stay with you afterwards?

It's always been with me, even before I was there. That is part of me because of who I am, who my father was, and my grandparents and my great-grandparents and all the way back.

> *"We were definitely inspired not simply by a screenplay but by a very real and very much living history."*

You've said you feel like this film is coming at the right time. Why?

Like most important work, it finds its time at the right time. I know with the *Malcolm X* film that I did with Spike Lee some years ago, it was the right people at the right time to tell that huge story; this undertaking is no less audacious. I knew the role of Isaiah would be a challenging one because it could be played on one level, but with the encouragement of Nate and all of our coworkers on *The Birth of a Nation*, I was encouraged to take Isaiah to several different levels of consciousness.

Every hero needs his or her foil, and I suppose that Isaiah is one of the great foils for Nat Turner. It's a conflict, it's a conversation, it's a debate that went on throughout the nineteenth century and certainly throughout the twentieth century, and it's certainly in the present moment; the central question in that debate is, *How do we get free?* What's the best way of liberating ourselves? That very heated conversation that Nat and Isaiah have in the cabin is a conversation that could very well be going on on the streets of Los Angeles, of Ferguson, or the streets of Brooklyn. People are trying to determine the best way of liberating—liberating themselves and their families and the community.

Playing Isaiah must have been an emotionally fraught experience for you. What did taking on this role mean for you?

It was about breathing that air and getting that mud on my boots. Nate is a Virginian. My father was a Virginian. We're both sons of Virginia, and we were both here to tell the quintessential Virginian story. It was a spiritual opening for me, a genealogical opening if you will, that led me to all of those moments that Isaiah had to live and breathe hopefully as someone we saw as a real person and not a stock character. I'd like to think Isaiah is definitely flesh and blood, and that I was able to inhabit him as such. But at the end of the day, I've have to take the boots off and go on with my life in the year of 2016. But that's what we do—that's the actor's world.

Principal Photography

Will stands marred and exhausted, his trembling legs struggling to support his body.

NAT regards the assembly, then turns to Earl, eyes averted.

NAT
(low)
Mr. Fowler, suh. Regarding my sermon, my plan is to foment in them concupiscence for song.

EARL
Concup what?

Samuel, out of earshot, looks on with growing concern.

NAT
Massa I'm askin' if you's opposed to me using singin' to keep yo' niggers down? As means to sing away any 'malignance.'

EARL FOWLER
That's fine. Ain't got no quarrel with singin'. Long as it don't interfere with they workin'.

NAT
Yes, suh. Thank you, suh.

Nat turns to the slaves, his subservience thaws, his jaw tightening slightly.

NAT (CONT'D)
Brethren... I pray you sing to the Lord a new song. Sing praise in the assembly of the righteous. Let the saints be joyful in glory; Let them sing aloud on their beds. Let the high praises of God be in the mouths of the saints, and a two-edged sword in their hand, to execute vengeance on the demonic nations, and punishments on those peoples!

Nat builds, as Samuel studies Earl, who watches on seemingly oblivious to Nat's innuendos.

NAT (CONT'D)
To bind their kings with chains, And their nobles with fetters of iron; To execute on them this written judgment–

118 CONTINUED:

NAT
Your earthly master is gone.
You are now free men and woman,
servants of only the Lord.

A murmur spreads throughout.

NAT (CONT'D)
As the sword of the Lord bears down
on our enemies, our ancestors and
unborn children rejoice.
(beat)
Are we dead? No. I say we are now
alive, seeing through eyes that
have been denied us since being
born into the darkness of bondage.
Stand with us... that your other
captive brothers and sisters may
also know freedom. Stand, that our
children, for generations to come
will know that with the
supernatural power of God, we
straightened our backs against the
works of the evil one.

A male steps forward. Then another. And other, until every
able man has stepped up. Off their determined looks-

119 EXT. WOODS - NIGHT 119

-- A group of torch-wielding REBELS gallop past camera.

120 INT. PLANTATION HOME - (NIGHT) 120

-- TIGHT ON A LIT WALL to reveal SHADOWS axing down on a bed.
BLOOD sprays against the wall with the last blow.

121 OMITTED 121

122 INT. PLANTATION HOME - (NIGHT) 122

-- Nat stands in a room of an estate, eyes a military sword
mounted on the wall. A REBEL and a SLAVEOWNER wrestle in the
BG.

NAT (O.S.)
And Mama.

CHERRY
She fine too.

Cherry shoots a nervous glance toward Catherine.

NAT (O.S.)
You heard anything on the others?

CHERRY
They been hanged... All of them.
They killing people everywhere. For
no reason at all, but being black.
Say the killin' won't stop til they
get you...
(then)
All this time, I thought... I
thought you were dead, too.

NAT (O.S.)
I'm here... I'll always be.

CHERRY
I miss you so much...

No answer. She stops.

CHERRY (CONT'D)
Nat?

CATHERINE (O.S.)
Cherry, who are you talking to?

Cherry turns to find Catherine just behind her. Cherry wipes her face. Catherine surveys the area, sees nothing.

CHERRY
I was just talking to myself...
wishing things was different.

Catherine regards her with compassion.

CATHERINE
Me too...

A long beat until-

Catherine pulls a wet shirt from the clothes basket, pins it to the line. They silently work in tandem.

PART V

Nat Turner Matters

Why Nat Turner Matters: *The Importance of History in Contemporary Consciousness*

by Brian Favors, M.Ed., *and*
Lurie Daniel Favors, Esq.

"Any psychiatrist can tell you that genuine healing requires a candid confrontation with our past. In any case, if there is to be reconciliation, first there must be truth."

—PROFESSOR TIM TYSON, AUTHOR, *BLOOD DONE SIGNED MY NAME*

"Go back and get it. It is not taboo to fetch what is at risk of being left behind."

—PRINCIPLE OF *SANKOFA*, FROM THE AKAN TRIBE, GHANA, WEST AFRICA

In recent years, dramas such as *Underground*, *Roots*, and *12 Years a Slave* have been well received. However, for many in our community, they can also be incredibly painful to watch. This truth has caused some to criticize the prevalence of "slave movies." While these critics make valid points, these stories, and those of heroes who resisted like Nat Turner, are important. They must continue to be told because they can empower us to understand, analyze, and heal from our current condition.

Some critics rightly note that with current black reality as challenging as it is, there's neither the desire nor the need to see additional scenes of black oppression. Considering the seemingly endless loop of black death and disenfranchisement that is often featured on local nightly news channels throughout the country, that is certainly a salient point.

Others point out that stories that start in slavery perpetuate the harmful lie that there weren't millennia-old, thriving, healthy African civilizations that predated the peculiar Western institution. This, too, is valid.

We typically do not learn anything about the depth of African history that predates Western slavery and colonization in our school system. Nor do we learn the truth about colonial exploitation and *what actually happened* to nearly destroy Africa. Without that knowledge, it can be hard to connect the dots between stories of ancient African glory and the conditions festering in Black America and throughout the continent of Africa currently.

Still others observe that institutions like the Academy Awards only bestow honors on black actors for playing slaves or other stereotypical, subservient roles. Add to this the fact that the way we as African-Americans learn American history often generates a sense of shame or pity that comes with the idea of having been someone's property (notably, there is rarely a sense of shame generated from having been an owner of another human being), and you realize these critics also have some merit.

But that's only part of the story.

The reality is we need many more stories that tell the true fullness about the experiences of enslaved Africans because these stories provide us with a lens to understand our current condition. That lens is vital to our ability to figure a way out.

Many of the challenges we face in the black community today—e.g., debates over use of the n-word, seemingly unchecked violence in our schools and communities, divisions over good and bad hair or light skin and dark skin, record unemployment and poverty, et cetera—were explicitly manufactured in the conditions created by race-based slavery and white supremacy. These wounds continue to fester today and can be so overwhelming that many feel powerless to heal them in any meaningful way. The ensuing sense of paralysis makes it that much more difficult to even *imagine* a Black community where these conditions *do not exist*.

Sadly, this harsh reality is compounded by the fact that far too few of us actually understand the roots from whence these issues came.

This is why stories about heroes like Nat Turner are so significant. His story is one of active resistance and engagement in the battle for freedom. That is an empowering paradigm shift.

Nat Turner's story converts the traditionally depressing narrative of slavery into one that gives us a road map for resistance and self-determination and makes the sentiments of Black Lives Matter a reality. Turner teaches us that in order to protect your people you have to love them enough to be willing to solve your collective problems on your own terms. In order for your life to *actually* matter, you have to be willing to die for the kind of freedom you desire.

After all, that's why America prides itself on holding up heroes like Patrick Henry, who declared "give me liberty or give me death" when faced with continued oppressive colonial rule.

Nat Turner's story is a reminder that Black lives do matter and that we can stand up on our own and create freedom on our own terms in ways that center on meeting our own needs.

The same way a doctor needs to know your medical history in order to properly treat you, we need to intimately know and understand our past so we can figure out how to properly treat our selves. We need stories that show the fullness of how slavery worked and its impact on our people; stories of the maroons, of resistance, of black family and of black love in spite of oppression. Not for Hollywood awards or for entertainment value, but because when we tell these stories, we can create a clear lens through which we can properly analyze, diagnose, and, most important, *heal* from our current condition.

Nat Turner's story is a reminder that Black lives do matter and that we can stand up on our own and create freedom on our own terms in ways that center on meeting our own needs.

When told from our perspective, these stories can become analytical decoders that not only explain *why* we're in the condition we're in but also give us a context for understanding how to address it. Most important, they remind us that freedom is never given and that we have the power to create our own solutions—on our own terms.

As educators, we know the power of changing the narrative of African enslavement from one of shame into one of resistance and innovation under extreme circumstances. We use these stories like *Roots*, *Underground*, and *12 Years a Slave* with our students to teach them how to employ the Akan principle of *sankofa*, which instructs us to look to our past so that we can understand our present and prepare for our future. We teach them to use these stories as tools to analyze what's happening in their communities right now so that we can create solutions that can heal us and our children going forward.

As Frederick Douglass once said, "The fact that we have endured wrongs and hardships, which would have destroyed any other race . . . ought to strengthen our faith that there is a better day coming, and that we by patience, industry, uprightness, and economy may hasten that better day."

When Black youth are empowered with this perspective, they are able to imagine what heroes like Harriet Tubman, Frederick Douglass, Sojourner Truth, and so many others would have been able to do if they had had access to the resources we have today. What more could Douglass have done with access to the Internet? What more could Tubman have done with Twitter or Facebook and access to other social media engagement? That dialogue can inspire young people and fill them with hope; it can help them transition from seeing the glass as half-empty to seeing it as half-full.

That's when the solutions and the healing can begin.

The story of Nat Turner, and stories of the struggles and triumphs of other enslaved African people, are only one small portion of the total Pan-African experience. But as they relate to the current state of affairs—these stories are powerfully salient tools in community healing and restoration. Nat Turner knew that Black lives mattered in the 1800s. The story of his dedication and sacrifice for his people can empower us to make that a reality today.

ACKNOWLEDGMENTS

My gratitude to the teams at Fox and 37 INK/Atria Books for working so diligently to bring this book to fruition. I'm particularly grateful to the production and design teams at Atria: Kimberly Goldstein, Dana Sloan, Jim Thiel, Navorn Johnson, Albert Tang, and freelance designer Jason Snyder. Thank you for your commitment to supporting my vision. Thank you, Judith Curr, for understanding the importance of this work and trusting the healing potential of this movement. I would like to thank Nancy Utley, Steve Gilula, and all of my Fox family who lent a hand in this process and continue to stand with me throughout this odyssey.

To the cast and crew who spoke with Briana Rodriguez and Dominic Patten, know that I appreciate your prioritizing this project. Your voices have elevated this work in more ways than you can imagine. For all of you whom I wasn't able to include, your energy is awash in the pictures and spirit of this effort.

I am in debt to the contributors, Daina Ramey Berry, Erica Armstrong Dunbar, Ruramai Musekiwa, Alfred Brophy, Kelley Fanto Deetz, Brian and Lurie Favors, Dominic Patten, Briana Rodriguez, Dwight Wilson II, and Jahi Chikwendiu. Erica Armstrong Dunbar, thanks for going above and beyond, doing so much more than was asked to ensure this project's integrity. To you all, your contributions give this book the truth and gravitas I had much hoped for.

Mollie Glick, you continue to strive far beyond the call of duty of a literary agent. Many thanks to you, Joy Fowlkes, and the rest of my hard-working CAA family.

Dawn Davis at 37 INK, you took a chance on a young writer. You guided and nurtured me throughout a process that often presented the steepest of learning curves. Thank you for your commitment and collaboration. You and Woody Dismukes were my constant guides.

To Krystle, Jisela, Norah, Mae-Lee, and Justice. You are the daddy fights.

Finally, thank you to my incredible wife, whose unyielding belief, devotion, and patience allowed me, through this journey, to reclaim and extend Nat Turner's legacy.

SUGGESTED READING

The Fires of Jubilee: Nat Turner's Fierce Rebellion by University of Massachusetts professor of History Stephen B. Oates

The Rebellious Slave: Nat Turner in American Memory by History professor Scot French

The Southampton Insurrection, published in the year 1900 by William Sidney Drewry, a rare work based on interviews with living witnesses

William Styron's Nat Turner: Ten Black Writers Respond edited by John Henrik Clarke

Post Traumatic Slave Syndrome: America's Legacy of Enduring Injury and Healing by psychologist Joy DeGruy

Nat Turner's Slave Rebellion: Including the 1851 "Confessions" by Herbert Aptheker

ABOUT THE CONTRIBUTORS

NATE PARKER is an award-winning actor, writer, director, and producer who has played lead characters and held starring roles in at least nineteen films, including *Beyond the Lights* and *Red Tails*. Parker's compelling portrayal of Henry Lowe in *The Great Debaters* earned him an NAACP Image Award nomination for best supporting actor. Parker wrote, directed, produced, and stars in *The Birth of a Nation*, which tells the story of Nat Turner (played by Parker) who famously led the 1831 slave rebellion in Virginia. In 2015, Parker launched the Nate Parker Foundation, which supports education, cultural enrichment, and social and economic justice. Parker holds a degree in Computer Programming from the University of Oklahoma and an honorary doctorate from Wiley College.

DAINA RAMEY BERRY is an associate professor of History and African and African Diaspora Studies at the University of Texas at Austin. She is the author of *Swing the Sickle for the Harvest Is Ripe: Gender and Slavery in Antebellum Georgia* (Illinois, 2007) and an award-winning editor of *Enslaved Women in America: An Encyclopedia* (ABC-Clio, 2012) and *Slavery and Freedom in Savannah* (UGA, 2014). Her scholarship has been supported by the National Endowment for the Humanities, the American Council of Learned Societies, the American Association of University Women, the Ford Foundation, and the College of Physicians of Philadelphia. She is also a distinguished lecturer for the Organization of American Historians. Berry's second single-authored book, titled *The Price for Their Pound of Flesh: The Value of the Enslaved from the Womb to the Grave in the Building of a Nation*, will be released in January 2017 (Beacon Press).

JAHI CHIKWENDIU, set photographer on *The Birth of a Nation*, has been a staff photographer with *The Washington Post* since 2001. A native of Lexington, Kentucky, and a former high school math teacher, Chikwendiu is affiliated with the National Association of Black Journalists (NABJ), the National Press Photographers Association (NPPA), and the White House News Photographers Association (WHNPA). Chikwendiu's work has been internationally recognized by the aforementioned organizations as well as Pictures of the Year International, World Press Photo, and the Overseas Press Club. His heart always comes back to the question of how to best evolve as a storyteller and how to best raise the next generation of visionaries.

ERICA ARMSTRONG DUNBAR is the Blue and Gold Professor of Black Studies and History at the University of Delaware. In 2011, Professor Dunbar was appointed the first director of the Program in African American History at the Library Company of Philadelphia. She has been the recipient of Ford, Mellon, and SSRC fellowships and is an Organization of American Historians distinguished lecturer. She is the author of *A Fragile Freedom: African American Women and Emancipation in the Antebellum City* (Yale, 2008) and has appeared in numerous documentaries, such as several episodes of *Philadelphia: The Great Experiment* as well as "The Abolitionists," an *American Experience* production on PBS. Her second book, *Never Caught: The Story of Ona Judge, the Washingtons' Runaway Slave*, will be published in February 2017 by 37 INK.

RURAMAI MUSEKIWA is a Zimbabwe-born graphic designer/visual artist by trade, with a background comprising fine art, desktop publishing, project management, and writing. Her most notable body of work is the acclaimed Sibahle (translated: "We Are Beautiful") poster series paying homage to phenomenal African women. She currently runs a social enterprise called Sibahle, which seeks to make use of creative mediums to challenge unhealthy mind-sets in African women and youth and foster collaboration among African creatives within the continent and diaspora, while driving profit through commercially viable products.

ALFRED L. BROPHY is the Judge John J. Parker Distinguished Professor of Law at the University of North Carolina at Chapel Hill. His books include *Reconstructing the Dreamland: The Tulsa Race Riot of 1921* (Oxford University Press, 2002), *Reparations Pro and Con* (Oxford University Press, 2006), and *University, Court, and Slave: Proslavery Thought in Southern Colleges and Courts and the Coming of Civil War* (Oxford University Press, 2016).

KELLEY FANTO DEETZ holds a B.A. in Black Studies from the College of William and Mary, as well as an M.A. in African-American Studies and a Ph.D. in African Diaspora Studies from the University of California at Berkeley. She specializes in nineteenth-century African-American culture, African diaspora archaeology, and public history (tourism, memorials, and memory). She is the former vice president and a current board member of the Legacy Museum of African American History in Lynchburg, Virginia, and the coeditor of the *African Diaspora Archaeology Newsletter*. She is currently working on a manuscript titled *Bound to the Fire: Virginia's Enslaved Cooks and Their Kitchens* (University of South Carolina Press), and her chapter "Stolen Bodies, Edible Memories: The Influence and Function of West African Foodways in the Early British Atlantic" will be in *The Routledge History of Food* due for publication in fall 2016.

DOMINIC PATTEN is the senior editor, legal and TV critic at *Deadline Hollywood*. Patten is not only responsible for breaking news about litigious Hollywood's major lawsuits and courtroom activities but also for offering insights on this new golden age of television with his video reviews and more. Additionally, Patten heads political coverage for *Deadline* and regularly posts stories on a wide variety of topics. He previously wrote for the *New York Times*, the *Los Angeles Times*, the *Washington Times*, and the *Globe and Mail*. A frequent guest on NPR, Fox News Channel, CNN, MSNBC, and CBS, Patten has been a documentary director, TV producer, national news correspondent, and newspaper editor.

BRIANA RODRIGUEZ is a native New Yorker covering the acting landscape across film, theater, and television. She's held the position of associate editor for *Backstage* and has written for *Billboard* and the Tribeca Film Institute.

BRIAN FAVORS, M.ED., AND LURIE DANIEL FAVORS, ESQ., are the co-founders of Breaking the Cycle Consulting Services, which specializes in training educators, parents, and youth to address the crisis in urban education through the use of culturally responsive teaching methods. Brian has a bachelor's degree in sociology from the University of California–Davis, an M.Ed. from Pennsylvania State University, and an M.S.Ed. from Queens College. He is the co-founder of the Nate Parker Foundation. Lurie has a bachelor's degree in African-American Studies from Pennsylvania State University and a Juris Doctorate from New York University School of Law. She currently serves as general counsel for the Center for Law and Social Justice at Medgar Evers College.

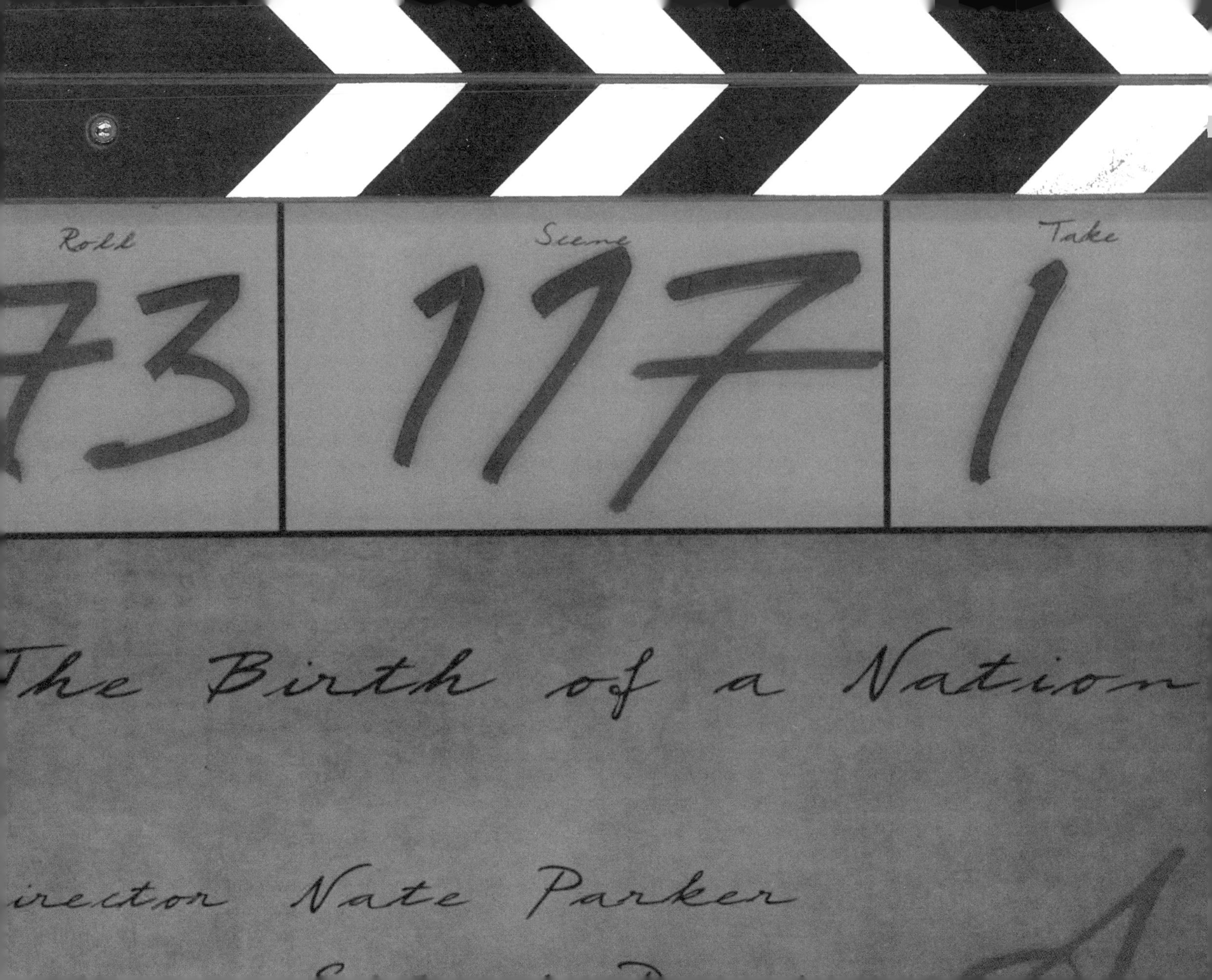

Roll
73
Scene
117
Take
1
The Birth of a Nation
irector Nate Parker